Revise for Edexcel
GCSE Resistant Materials

Barry Lambert

D1146476

Series Editor: Chris Weaving

Wycliffe College	Design & Technology Centre				
Name	Date	A	B	C	D	E

Success through qualifications

Heinemann Educational Publishers
Halley Court, Jordan Hill, Oxford OX2 8EJ
Part of Harcourt Education

Heinemann is the registered trademark of
Harcourt Education Limited

© Barry Lambert and Chris Weaving, 2003

First published 2003
07 06 05 04 03
10 9 8 7 6 5 4 3 2 1

British Library Cataloguing in Publication Data is available
from the British Library on request.

ISBN 0 435 41720 7

Designed and typeset by Techset, Tyne and Wear

Original illustrations © Harcourt Education Limited, 2003

Illustrated by Techset, Tyne and Wear

Printed in The Bath Press Ltd, Bath

Cover photo: © Gareth Boden, Imagebank and Ace Photo Library

Acknowledgements
Every effort has been made to contact copyright holders of material reproduced in this book. Any omissions will be
rectified in subsequent printings if notice is given to the publishers.

Tel: 01865 888058 email: info.he@heinemann.co.uk

CONTENTS

If yes read on...

What is revision?

Revision in preparation for an examination is defined as *reviewing previously learned material*.

Why revise?

The purpose of revision is to:

- *refresh your knowledge and understanding* of previously learned material;
- *improve your ability to recall and apply this knowledge and understanding* to the questions on the examination paper.

How can revision improve my grade?

The written examination paper:

- is worth 40% of the whole examination (the other 60% comes from coursework);
- has four questions, each worth 10% of the whole examination.

Therefore, thorough revision that enables four questions to be answered well, can earn a large proportion of these marks and contribute significantly to the final grade awarded.

Do I need to know about all the content listed in the Exam Board Specification?

Yes because:

- the examination board will test all content listed in the Specification at least once during its life (normally five years);
- if something has been tested once, it does not mean it will not be tested again in a future exam paper.

It is therefore essential that you prepare fully by revising everything listed in the Specification.

How does this book help me?

It has been written by examiners who know:

- how the questions are written;
- what is needed in the answers.

What does the book tell me?

The book contains important information about the examination paper and about what you need to know.

1 Section 1 tells you about the examination paper:
- how it is structured;
- how part questions are structured;
- the importance of *Key Words* in each part question;
- how to manage your time answering the questions;
- how to write your answers to access all of the marks.

2 Section 2 and Section 3:
- combine some content headings from the Examination Board Specification to form single *Topic* headings;
- show how these content headings must be integrated when applied to designing;
- help you to understand how to apply the knowledge and understanding, you already have, to designing;
- help you focus your revision and make more effective use of that time.

3 Section 4 helps you to:
- understand the *Design Question* (not Short Course);
- understand the *Product Analysis Question*.
- recognise the types of part questions that may be included;
- recognise what is needed to answer each question successfully by giving sample answers.

Do the *Topics* tell me what I need to know to answer the exam questions?

Yes. These *Topics*:

- are introduced by identifying the major areas of the Specification content for which you need to have an appropriate level of knowledge and understanding;
- expand this content into *Key Points*.

What do the *Key Points* tell me?

The *Key Points*:

- identify the detail of what you need to know;
- focus the detail towards its application in product design and make/manufacture i.e. how different materials properties present design opportunities and how different making/manufacturing processes present design opportunities.

What about industrial applications?

The industrial applications icon will show where industrial processes are addressed within each *Topic*.

Are there any sample questions and answers?

Yes. Each *Topic* will include sample part questions, complete with full answers to show:

- how questions might be asked;
- the depth and breadth of knowledge and understanding required;
- how to present answers to access all of the marks.

 This icon indicates industrial applications

 This icon indicates information not required for the Short Course

Section 1
Revision strategy and explanation

THE QUESTION PAPER

Short course (SC)

There will be two different question papers: one each for the foundation and higher tiers. For the examination you will be given one of these papers.

The question paper will be marked out of a total of 44 marks.

The time for answering the paper is 1 hour.

All questions are compulsory and must be answered in the spaces provided on the question paper.

Each question paper will have three separate questions as follows:

- Two questions will test specific knowledge and understanding from AO1* and will be worth 11 marks each (see further guidance in this section and Section 2).
- One question will test product analysis AO3* (iii) and will be worth 22 marks (see Sections 3 and 4).

* AO1 and AO3 are the Assessment Objectives listed in Edexcel's Subject Specification booklet. They contain the knowledge and understanding that the examination questions will be based upon. Section 2 of this book deals with AO1 and Section 3 deals with AO3.

 xaminer's Tip

To score as many marks as you are able, you must attempt all questions and part questions.

Full course (FC)

There will be two different question papers, one each for the foundation and higher tiers. For the examination you will be given one of these papers.

The question paper will be marked out of a total of 88 marks.

The time for answering the paper is $1\frac{1}{2}$ hours.

All questions are compulsory and must be answered in the spaces provided on the question paper.

Each question paper will have four separate questions as follows:

- One question, 22 marks, will test specific knowledge and understanding from AO1* (see further guidance in this section).
- The first half of another question, 11 marks, will test different specific knowledge and understanding from AO1*, with the second half testing specific knowledge and understanding from AO3* (i) and (ii), 11 marks (see further guidance in this section and Sections 2 and 3).
- The design question, 22 marks, will test AO2* (see Section 4).
- The product analysis question, 22 marks, will test AO3 (iii) (see Section 4).

* AO1, AO2 and AO3 are the Assessment Objectives listed in Edexcel's Subject Specification booklet. AO1 and AO3 contain the knowledge and understanding that the examination questions will be based upon. Section 2 of this book deals with AO1 and Section 3 deals with AO3.

xaminer's Tip

To score as many marks as you are able, you must attempt all questions and part questions.

Short course and Full course (SC/FC)

Each separate question will be divided into smaller part questions labelled (a), (b), (c), etc. These part questions are likely to be progressively more difficult.

Alphabetically labelled part questions, for example (a), may also be divided further into smaller parts and these are labelled (i), (ii), (iii), etc. These smaller parts will all be linked to the common theme of this part question.

The marks available for each part question are shown at the end of that part question, for example **(2 marks)**.

xaminer's Tip

These marks also suggest how long you should spend answering each question. For example, you should spend approximately twice as long thinking about and answering a question worth 2 marks compared to answering a question worth 1 mark.

On all question papers the potentially easier questions will be towards the beginning of the paper, with those that are potentially more difficult towards the end. This also usually applies to the part questions within a whole question, that is, there is an increase in difficulty between the beginning and end of the paper and between the beginning and end of each question.

xaminer's Tip

Make sure each answer fully satisfies the question set. That is, if you give simple one-word answers to the more valuable questions, you will not score many marks.

How you should answer individual questions

Each part question will use a key word to tell you the type of answer that is required. Some key words and answer types are as follows:

Key words	Answer type
Give State Name	Normally a one- or two-word answer, at the very most a short sentence.
Name the specific	As above, but requires specific detail to be given. Generic answers such as 'wood' or 'plastic' will gain no marks.

Describe	Normally, one or two sentences which form a description, making reference to more than one point. All points must be linked for a complete answer.
Explain	Normally, one or two sentences which form an explanation. This requires a clear or detailed account of something and includes a relevant justification, reason or example.
Use notes and sketches ⎫ Annotated sketches ⎬	Mainly a sketched answer with notes to support or clarify particular points in the answer. 'Sketch' means 'a quick freehand drawing'. Marks are awarded for the accuracy of the technical information communicated in the answer rather than the drawing skills shown.
Evaluate	Normally one or two sentences where the quality, suitability or value of something is judged. This can include both positive and negative points, with each point normally requiring a relevant justification, reason or example.

 xaminer's Tip

The number of pieces of information required in any answer will be shown by the number of marks given to the part question.

 xaminer's Tip

The space given on the question paper suggests the maximum that you should write or draw in answer to any question.

 xaminer's Tip

No marks are given for repeating information given in the question.

 xaminer's Tip

Where / is used in an example answer it means that what follows is an alternative to the part of the answer that precedes it, not an addition.

The following example questions and answers illustrate the use of the main key words in part questions and the different style and length of answers required.

Q1 *Manufacturers buy components, such as screws, as a standard component.*

(i) *Give **two** advantages to the manufacturer, of using standard components.*

1 ....

2 ....

(2 marks)

A full answer requires two different advantages to the manufacturer to be stated. For example:

1 No need for specialist machinery equipment to make the screw.

2 Consistent quality of component established by the supplier.

Q2 *Describe **one** advantage to the environment of using plastics which are suitable for recycling.*

....

....

(2 marks)

A full answer for 2 marks requires a statement containing two linked points, as shown below in **bold text**. For example:

Recycling plastic means that **fewer raw materials** are used with the result that the **earth's resources will last longer**.

Q3 *Explain the importance of **two** safety issues which designers must consider when designing toys for young children.*

1 ....

....

2 ....

....

(4 marks)

A full answer for 4 marks requires two different safety issues to be identified and the importance of each to be explained or justified. For example:

1 It must be made from **non-toxic materials** because a child **must not be poisoned** if they put the toy in their mouth.

2 It **must not have small detachable parts** because of the **risk of a child swallowing** one.

(E)xaminer's Tip

Note that both of these answers have two parts to them, each linked by the word 'because'.

Section 2
Assessment
objective 1

MATERIALS PROCESSING: PRIMARY MATERIALS AND PRIMARY PROCESSING TO STANDARD FORMS

TOPICS

You need to know:

☐ that hardwoods and softwoods are natural timbers

☐ that primary materials are processed to produce standard stock sizes and sections

☐ about the characteristics and applications of hardwoods and softwoods.

KEY POINTS

NATURAL TIMBERS

Hardwoods and softwoods are natural. Timbers are classified as follows:

Hardwoods	Softwoods
Oak	Pine
Mahogany	
Beech	
Ash	
Birch	

PRIMARY MATERIALS

Primary materials are processed to produce standard stock sizes and sections suitable for manufacturing into products. This range of sizes allows designers to see what is available before they start designing. Using standard stock sizes can reduce costs later as the timber will not need machining to specific sizes.

Secondary processing can take the form of:

* cutting
* planing
* drilling
* shaping.

CHARACTERISTICS AND APPLICATIONS OF HARDWOODS AND SOFTWOODS

Timber	Hard/soft	Origin	Properties/ characteristics	Uses
Oak	Hardwood	Europe, USA	• Hard and tough • Durable • Finishes well • Heavy • Contains an acid which corrodes steel	• High quality furniture • Garden benches • Boat building • Veneers
Mahogany	Hardwood	Central and South America	• Easy to work • Durable • Finishes well • Prone to warping (going out of shape)	• Indoor furniture • Interior woodwork • Window frames • Veneers
Beech	Hardwood	Europe	• Hard and tough • Finishes well • Prone to warping • Turns well	• Workshop benches • Children's toys • Interior furniture
Ash	Hardwood	Europe	• Tough • Flexible (good elastic properties) • Works and finishes well	• Sports equipment • Ladders • Laminated furniture • Tool handles
Birch	Hardwood	Europe	• Hard wearing	• Plywood veneers
Pine (Scots)	Softwood	Northern Europe	• Easy to work • Knotty and prone to warping	• Constructional wood work (joists, roof trusses) • Floorboards • Children's toys

The properties and characteristics of timbers can be categorized by their:

• colour   • grain   • texture   • figure   • hardness   • elasticity.

The mechanical strength of a wood is dependent upon how compact the cells are. Hardwood cells are more compact than softwood cells. Hardwoods generally have greater mechanical strength and hardness in comparison to softwoods.

Examination questions

 Q1 *Name **two** different hardwoods that could be used in the production of a dining room table.*

 2 marks

Acceptable answer

Oak and mahogany.

 Examiner's Tip

Name will only require a one- or two-word answer, at the very most a short sentence.

Q2 *Describe **one** advantage of using veneers rather than using solid timber.*

2 marks

Acceptable answer

Using veneers means that **fewer trees will have to be cut down** because the thinner **veneers can be used to cover** cheaper manufactured boards/go further.

 Examiner's Tip

A full answer for 2 marks requires a statement containing two linked points as shown on the left.

TOPICS

You need to know:

☐ about the range of manufactured boards available

☐ the advantages and disadvantages of using manufactured boards

☐ about the characteristics and uses of manufactured boards.

KEY POINTS

RANGE OF MANUFACTURED BOARDS AVAILABLE

The mass production of furniture is almost entirely based around the use of manufactured board.

Manufactured boards fall into the following categories:

- MDF (medium density fibreboard)
- plywood
- hardboard
- blockboard
- chipboard.

ADVANTAGES AND DISADVANTAGES OF USING MANUFACTURED BOARDS

Advantages	Disadvantages
Available in large sheets	Blunt tools quickly
Good dimensional stability	Thin sheets flop if not supported
Easily decorated	Difficult to join
Easily bent and shaped over formers	Edges must be concealed
Waste products can be used in the making of manufactured boards	Cutting and sanding of some boards can generate hazardous dust particles

THE CHARACTERISTICS AND USES OF MANUFACTURED BOARDS

Board	Characteristics	Uses
Medium density fibreboard	MDF is very widely used in mass-produced, flat-packed furniture. It is a very dense material with an excellent surface finish, which can be veneered or painted. It is very stable and is not affected by changing humidity levels.	• Flat-pack furniture • Drawer bottoms • Kitchen units • Heat and sound insulation
Plywood	This board is made up from an odd number of layers (veneers) normally 1.5 mm thick. The grain of each layer is at right angles to the layer either side of it. The two outside layers run in the same direction. Plywood is very strong in all directions and it is also very resistant to splitting. Birch veneers are usually used on the outside layers resulting in an attractive surface.	• Boat building (exterior quality plywood) • Drawer bottoms and wardrobe bottoms • Tea chests • Cheaper grades used in construction industry for hoardings and shuttering
Chipboard	This board is made from waste products. It is bonded together using very strong resins. Although it has no grain pattern, it is equally strong in all directions but not as strong as plywood. The surface is generally veneered or covered with a plastic laminate. It is not very resistant to water although special moisture resistant grades are available.	• Large floor boards and decking for loft spaces • Shelving • Kitchen worktops • Flat-pack furniture
Blockboard	This board has long strips of timber running down its length. A veneer is applied to the external surface. It does not possess uniform strength.	• Fire doors • Tabletops
Hardboard	This is the cheapest of the manufactured boards. It is made from compressed fibres that have been soaked in a resin before being compressed. One side is very smooth and the underside is textured. It is unsuitable for external use because it absorbs moisture easily.	• Drawer bottoms • Cabinet backs • Smoothing out uneven floors • Lightweight internal door cladding

Examination question

 *Explain **one** reason which makes hardboard unsuitable for outside use.*

2 marks

Acceptable answer

Hardboard is unsuitable for outside use because it is **not waterproof**.
Therefore it will **absorb water and will eventually rot and break down**.

Manufactured boards

THE DIFFERENCE BETWEEN FERROUS AND NON-FERROUS METALS

TOPICS

You need to know:

☐ that metals are classified as ferrous, non-ferrous or as alloys

☐ what the term alloy means.

KEY POINTS

METALS ARE CLASSIFIED AS FERROUS, NON-FERROUS OR AS ALLOYS

Ferrous	Alloys		Non-ferrous
Iron	Can be either ferrous or non-ferrous		Copper
			Tin
			Lead
			Zinc

An alloy is made by combining two or more metallic elements to make a new material with improved properties such as hardness or tensile strength, e.g. steel, brass.

Metals are an ideal material for use in mass production. They can be:

- bent
- welded
- stretched
- cut
- drilled
- twisted
- cast
- folded
- riveted
- pressed.

STEEL – A FERROUS ALLOY

Steel is an alloy of iron and carbon. Mild steel, stainless steel and silver steel are all ferrous alloys. Only a small amount of carbon (0.3 per cent) in iron will change the mechanical properties significantly.

Other elements such as chromium and vanadium can be introduced to improve resistance to corrosion. A small addition of silver will improve its ability to retain a cutting edge and this material – silver steel – is often used for cutting tools and kitchen implements.

Iron and steel

Metal	Composition	Properties/characteristics	Uses
Iron	Pure metal	• Soft and ductile • Weak in tension	• Alloyed with carbon to make steel
Mild steel	Alloy of iron and carbon (0.15 – 0.3% carbon)	• Tough, ductile and malleable • Good tensile strength • Easily joined by welding or brazing • Poor resistance to corrosion • Cannot be easily heat treated • Easily worked in school workshop	• Structural steel girders • Car body panels • Nails, screws, nuts and bolts, general ironmongery
Stainless steel	Alloy of steel (12% chromium, 8% nickel)	• Hard and tough • Excellent resistance to corrosion • Difficult to use in school workshop	• Cutlery • Kitchen sinks • Pots and pans
Silver steel	Alloy of steel (0.8 – 1.5% carbon)	• Very hard and less ductile than mild steel • Difficult to cut but easily joined by welding	• Scribers • Screwdriver blades

BRASS – A NON-FERROUS ALLOY

Brass is a non-ferrous alloy and has improved resistance to corrosion. It also casts and turns easily and is therefore ideal as a material for boat and plumbing fittings.

Examination questions

 Q1 *Describe **two** advantages of making alloys.* **4 marks**

Acceptable answer

Alloys can have **improved mechanical properties** such as **greater hardness/toughness**.

The **physical properties can be improved** such as **increasing a material's resistance to corrosion**.

Q2 *Stainless steel is hard and tough. It also has excellent resistance to corrosion. Give **two** uses of stainless steel.* **2 marks**

Acceptable answers

Cutlery/kitchen sinks/pots and pans.

You need to know:

☐ about the heat treatment of metals

☐ about the various heat treatment processes.

KEY POINTS

HEAT TREATMENT

Heat treatment refers to the process of heating and cooling metals in a controlled manner.

Heat treatment processes are carried out to change the properties of the metals.

The five main heat treatment processes are:

- annealing
- normalizing
- hardening
- tempering
- case-hardening.

VARIOUS PROCESSES

ANNEALING

Annealing involves heating up the metal to a certain temperature and then allowing it to cool. This process is carried out on metal or components that have been deformed by bending, rolling or hammering. As a result of these processes the hardness of the metal has been increased and it becomes increasingly more difficult to work. The annealing process relieves the internal stresses created and makes it easier to work again.

NORMALIZING

Normalizing is a process only applied to steel. The grain structure becomes coarse as a result of work hardening and it must be normalized to restore its ductility and toughness.

The process of normalizing involves heating the metal to a temperature between 700°C and 900°C and soaked at that temperature for a short while before being allowed to cool in still air.

HARDENING

Only steel that has 0.4 per cent of carbon in it can be hardened. The full effect of hardening is only possible if the carbon content is above 0.8 per cent.

For steel to be used to make scribers, punches and drills it must be possible to fully harden the steel. Hardening is carried out by heating it to a cherry-red colour, and holding it at this temperature to ensure a uniform temperature before quenching it in water. At this point, the material will be very hard but also very brittle. The hardness must be reduced a little through the process of tempering.

TEMPERING

Firstly, the piece of steel to be tempered must be polished. This will allow the oxide film to be seen on the surface as the component is reheated. As the piece is reheated the colour film moves along the component and when the required colour reaches the tip, it should be quenched in water. The process of tempering will have reduced the hardness and brittleness of the component.

Tempering colour chart

Approx. temperature (°C)	Colour	Toughness		Uses
230	Pale straw	least		Lathe tools
240	Straw			Scribers
250	Dark straw			Centre punch
260	Brown			Tin snips
270	Brown-purple			Scissors
280	Purple			Saw blades
290	Dark purple		↓	Screw driver
300	Blue	most		Springs

CASE-HARDENING

Mild steel can only be hardened by case-hardening. This gives it a carbon-rich skin on the outside while retaining the more elastic, ductile properties on the inside.

The component should be heated to cherry red and then dipped into a carbon powder. This process should be repeated three times before quenching it in water on the final occasion.

Examination question

 a *Describe the process of hardening a piece of silver steel.*

2 marks

Acceptable answer

The piece of silver steel is **heated to a cherry-red colour** and held at this temperature to soak before being **quenched in water or oil**.

---

b *As a result of hardening the piece of silver steel, it has become too hard and brittle. Name the heat treatment process which must be used to reduce the brittleness from the hardened component.*

1 mark

Acceptable answer

Tempering

THE DIFFERENCE BETWEEN THERMOPLASTICS AND THERMOSETTING PLASTICS

You need to know:

☐ that plastics are classified into thermoplastics and thermosetting plastics

☐ about the properties and uses of thermoplastics and thermosetting plastics.

KEY POINTS

CLASSIFICATION OF PLASTICS

Plastics are classified into the following categories:

Thermoplastics	Thermosetting plastics
Acrylic	Epoxy resin
Polythene – low density; high density	
ABS	
Polyester	

Most plastics are derived from crude oil. The oil is processed in a fractioning tower where it is split into various compounds and materials.

Plastics are divided into the two basic categories – thermoplastics and thermosetting plastics – depending upon the way in which the chains are formed.

THERMOPLASTICS

- Thermoplastics have long chains which are tangled together in no formal pattern.
- They have very few cross links which means that when heated they become soft allowing them to be bent, pressed and formed into different shapes.
- They become stiff again as they cool.

THERMOSETTING PLASTICS

- Thermosetting plastics are made up from long chains of molecules that are cross linked.
- They have a very rigid structure.
- Once heated, thermosetting plastics can be moulded, shaped and pressed into shapes.
- Once set, they cannot be reheated since they are permanently set.

PROPERTIES AND USES OF THERMOPLASTICS AND THERMOSETTING PLASTICS

Plastic	Type	Properties/characteristics	Uses
Acrylic	Thermoplastic	• Stiff, hard and durable • Easily scratched • Good electrical insulator • Available in a wide range of colours • Polishes and finishes well	• Baths and bathroom furniture • Car indicator covers/reflectors
Polythene (low density) – LDPE	Thermoplastic	• Tough • Resistant to chemicals • Soft and flexible • Good electrical insulator • Available in a wide range of colours	• Squeezy bottles for shampoo and washing-up liquid • Toys • Carrier bags
Polythene (high density) – HDPE	Thermoplastic	• Stiffer and harder than LDPE • Surface has a waxy feel to it • Can be sterilized • Good resistance to corrosion	• Buckets • Bowls • Milk crates • Bleach bottles
ABS	Thermoplastic	• High impact strength • Lightweight and durable • Resistant to chemicals • High quality of surface finish	• Telephones • Kitchenware • Toys
Polyester	Thermoplastic	• Stiff, hard and brittle • Very resilient when laminated with GRP (glass reinforced plastic) • Good heat and chemical resistance	• Product cases such as hair dryers • Paperweight castings • Boat hulls with GRP
Epoxy resin	Thermosetting plastic	• Good resistance to wear and chemicals • High strength when used as a bonding agent on **fibrous** materials	• Adhesives • PCB (printed circuit board) material • Lamination of woven sheets such as fibre glass

Examination question

 Describe **one** difference between the structure of thermoplastics and thermosetting plastics.

2 marks

Acceptable answer

Thermosetting plastics have **cross-linked chains which make them stiff** whereas thermoplastic plastics have **long tangled chains making them more soft and flexible**.

Examiner's Tip

A full answer for 2 marks requires a statement containing two linked points.

COMPONENTS AND FIXINGS; GLUES AND ADHESIVES

You need to know:

☐ about the various adhesives available and their applications

☐ about and understand health and safety issues relating to their use.

KEY POINTS

BASIC ADHESIVES

There are five basic adhesives used in the school workshop. They are:

- PVA
- cascamite
- contact adhesives
- epoxy resins
- Tensol cement

All joints made with adhesives are permanent and it is essential that the correct adhesive is used for the specific materials being joined. When using adhesives the gluing or contact area should be as large as possible.

ADHESIVES' APPLICATIONS

Polyvinyl acetate (PVA)
- General woodworking adhesive
- A waterproof type is available
- Must be a good tight fitting joint
- Joint needs to be held under pressure while adhesive cures

Cascamite
- Waterproof woodworking adhesive used in boat building and exterior garden furniture
- Can be used to fill small gaps
- Joint needs to be held under pressure while adhesive cures

Contact adhesive
- Adhesive sticks on contact
- Applied to both surfaces
- Can stick different materials – wood to metal sheet, plastic to wood
- Must be used in a well-ventilated area because of the fumes it gives off

Epoxy resin (Araldite)
- Versatile but expensive
- Can be used to bond almost any clear, dry material
- Two-part adhesive which must be mixed
- Full strength achieved after two to three days

Tensol cement
- Used for acrylic only
- Chemical reaction with surface
- Must try to make contact/gluing area as large as possible
- Should be used in a well-ventilated area

Examination questions

Q1   *Name a general purpose woodworking adhesive.*

Acceptable answer

PVA

Q2   *State the correct adhesive to use when joining two pieces of acrylic together.*

Acceptable answer

Tensol cement.

Q3   *Both contact adhesives and Tensol cement give off dangerous fumes and can be harmful to your health.*

*Give **two** safety precautions that must be taken when using either contact adhesives or Tensol cement.*

Acceptable answers

It must be used in a well-ventilated area.
Care should be taken to avoid any contact with the skin or splashes to the eyes.

You need to know:

☐ how nails, nuts and bolts are used

☐ how to use screws

☐ about and understand the use of springs and hinges.

KEY POINTS

NAILS, SCREWS AND NUTS AND BOLTS

Nails, screws and nuts and bolts offer a quick and effective method of joining woods and metals.

Nails:
- grip the wood fibres as they are driven into the wood
- are difficult to withdraw
- are sold according to length and type.

Nuts and bolts:
- provide a temporary fixture
- are available in various forms but generally with a head which is hexagonal in shape
- are generally made from high tensile steel.

Washers should be used in between nuts and bolts to protect the surface and to help distribute the load.

Screws:
- are neat, strong and can be removed easily
- are classified by their length, gauge, type of head and material.

When using brass screws, a steel screw should be inserted first.

HOW TO USE SCREWS

Wood screws offer a strong and neat method of fixing wood. They can be removed easily and are therefore temporary unless they are used with an adhesive.

It is important to follow these tips when using screws to avoid splitting the wood or damaging the screw head.

1 Screw through the thinnest piece into the thicker one.

2 The screw should be three times as long as the piece being fixed.

3 Drill a clearance hole through the piece being joined slightly bigger than the shank of the screw.

4 Either drill a pilot hole or make one with a bradawl.

5 Use a countersink drill to make a countersunk recess.

6 If using brass screws in hardwood, use a steel screw of the same size first. Then replace it with a brass screw.

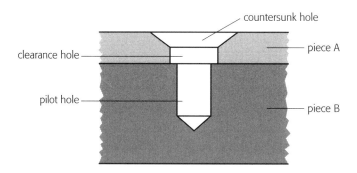

SPRINGS AND HINGES

Springs are used to:

- control movement
- limit impacts
- apply forces
- reduce vibration
- measure forces.

Springs are grouped into two categories:

- Compression springs shorten under a load and have their ends ground to provide a flat seat.
- Tension springs have pre-tensioned hooks on their ends so that a small load opens the coils.

Hinges allow doors to move and open. The butt hinge is the most widely used. One leaf or flap is screwed into a recess cut in the frame while the other is recessed into the door.

Examination questions

 a *Give the correct name for the type of screw shown below.*

A

b *Name the part of the screw labelled A on the diagram above.*

1 mark

Acceptable answer

a Countersunk head

b Shank

---

 *Explain **two** reasons why washers should be used when using nuts and bolts.*

2 marks

Acceptable answer

Reason 1: They help to **spread the load** more evenly **over the surface of the work**

Reason 2: They help to **protect the surface** of the work which is being **bolted together**.

Q3 *Explain **one** reason why brass screws should be used in products that will be left outside.*

2 marks

Acceptable answer

Brass screws should be used on outside products because they **will not rust like steel** and therefore the product **will remain fixed together and it will not fall apart**.

KNOCK-DOWN FITTINGS

You need to know:

☐ about the use of knock-down fittings and structural items.

KEY POINTS

KNOCK-DOWN FITTINGS AND STRUCTURAL ITEMS

Knock-down joints allow strong joints to be made quickly and easily. The parts can be taken apart so that the whole product can be 'knocked down' and flat packed.

The most common form of knock-down fitting is a nylon joint block. These are screwed into the corners.

More sophisticated fittings are available such as a machine screw and a metal dowel which is threaded.

Shelving systems can be either:

• fixed, or

• adjustable.

The adjustable type have the obvious advantage over a fixed system because the spacing between them can be adjusted to suit individual needs.

Angle tee plates are fixing and joining plates pressed from steel. They are used to create a fixing at either corner joints or tee joints.

Examination question

 a Explain **one** advantage for the consumer of products that make use of knock-down fittings in their construction.

2 marks

b Explain **one** different advantage for the manufacturer of products that make use of knock-down fittings in their construction.

2 marks

Acceptable answer

a The flatpack product is generally **small enough** to fit into the back of the car for **easy transportation**.

b The storage space needed in the warehouse is **much smaller** since the products are flat and not assembled.

 Examiner's Tip

A full answer for a total of 4 marks requires one different advantage to be identified for both the consumer and manufacturer.

PROPERTIES AND WORKING CHARACTERISTICS OF MATERIALS

You need to understand:

☐ the choices involved in selecting materials

☐ the aesthetic, physical and mechanical properties of materials.

KEY POINTS

SELECTION OF MATERIALS

Designers must be aware of the properties and limitations of the materials they intend to use. The properties of materials can be classified as either mechanical or physical.

The best and most appropriate choice of material depends on many factors, including:

- its mechanical/physical properties
- its aesthetic qualities
- the cost of both material and production
- its availability.

A small change in any one of the above may have a significant effect in other areas.

Although it is crucial that products function correctly and safely, it is also important that the designs 'look good'. These qualities which make designs attractive determine the product's aesthetic appeal.

AESTHETIC PROPERTIES

Aesthetic judgments can be broken down into:

- shape and form
- texture
- colour.

MECHANICAL AND PHYSICAL PROPERTIES

Mechanical properties are associated with how a material behaves when subjected to a force. Physical properties are not associated with the application of a force.

Mechanical	Physical
Compression	Density
Tension	Corrosion resistance
Hardness	Electrical resistance/insulation
Toughness	Fusability
Elasticity	Thermal insulation
Plasticity	Optical properties
Durability	Durability

Physical and mechanical properties of metals

Property	Physical/ mechanical	Description	Material	Applications
Electrical conductivity	Physical	Low resistance to the flow of an electric current	Gold, silver, copper and aluminium	Electrical cable
Thermal conductivity	Physical	Measure of how much heat travels through a material	Metals generally, but copper especially	Car radiators
Thermal insulator	Physical	Materials which have a low value of thermal conductivity	Non-metals generally	Cavity wall insulation
Fusibility	Physical	Ability to change into a liquid or molten state at a certain temperature	Tin Lead Aluminium	Solder Castings Alloys
Density	Physical	The mass per unit volume kg/m^3	High – lead Low – expanded polystyrene	Fishing weights Buoyancy aids
Optical	Physical	Materials react to light in different ways – reflection and absorption	Wood is opaque Glass is transparent	Acrylic reflector lenses for cars
Strength	Mechanical	There are five types: • tensile • compressive • bending • shear • torsion	Materials behave in different ways when subjected to different forces	Grades of steel have been developed to resist these different types of forces
Elasticity	Mechanical	Ability to return to original shape after force has been removed	Spring steel Rubber Ash	Springs Sports racket handles
Plasticity	Mechanical	Ability to be changed permanently without cracking or breaking	Acrylic ABS	Baths Plastic moulded products
Ductility	Mechanical	Ability to be drawn or stretched	Silver Copper	Electrical cables
Malleability	Mechanical	Ability to be deformed by compression without tearing or cracking	Lead	Roof flashing
Hardness	Mechanical	Ability to withstand abrasive wear and indentation	High carbon steel Silver steel	Drills Files Scribers
Toughness	Mechanical	Ability to withstand sudden shock loading without fracture	Mild steel	Nails Screws Car body panels
Durability	Mechanical/ physical	Ability to withstand weathering deterioration and corrosion	Plastics generally Gold	Window frames Jewellery

Examination questions

 a *Name a material that is tough.*

1 mark

b *Give **one** example of a product or component that needs to be tough.*

1 mark

Acceptable answer
a Mild steel
b Car body panels

 Explain the difference between an electrical insulator and an electrical conductor.

2 marks

Acceptable answer
An electrical conductor is a material which has a **low resistance** and therefore **will allow a current to flow** through it whereas an insulator has a **high electrical resistance** and **will not allow a current to flow** through it.

Q3 *The drawing below shows a saucepan.*

a *Name a specific material suitable for the handle.*

1 mark

b *Describe one property that makes it suitable for use when cooking food.*

2 marks

Acceptable answer
a Any natural timber would be acceptable, e.g. beech, ash.
b The material for the pan should be a **good conductor of heat** so that it **quickly heats the food** being cooked within it.

Q4 *Density is a physical property. In certain situations, materials are chosen for applications where they need to be very dense or to exhibit very low density.*

    a *State* **one** *material which is very dense and* **one** *material which is not very dense.*

    b *Give an application for each of the materials you have named in your answer to* **(a)** *above.*

Acceptable answers

a   High density   Lead or steel
     Low density   expanded polystyrene

b   Application of high density materials   fishing weights
     Application of low density materials   buoyancy aids

Q5 *Copper is a good electrical conductor and as such it is used extensively in electrical cables.*

Name another property which copper exhibits.

Acceptable answer

Ductility – the ability to be drawn or stretched.

TOPICS

You need to know:

☐ that the choice of material depends upon a number of factors.

KEY POINTS

SELECTION AND CHOICE OF MATERIAL

The selection and choice of material must be carefully considered for each product or component. The following five key factors should be taken into account:

- the working properties of the material
- the relevant manufacturing processes
- the range of appropriate finishes
- the dimensional accuracy of the finished product
- the cost of the material.

All of the above points need to be considered regardless of whether the product is a one-off, batch produced or made in high volumes.

Examination question

Q1 *The diagram shows a plastic drinks bottle.*

a *Name a specific type of plastic suitable for manufacturing the bottle.*

Acceptable answer

Polythene

10,000 identical bottles are required.

b *Give the name of the manufacturing process which would be used to produce the main body of the bottle.*

Acceptable answer

Blow moulding

CHOICE AND FITNESS FOR PURPOSE (2)

You need to understand:

☐ the relationship between working properties and the choice of material.

KEY POINTS

WORKING PROPERTIES AND CHOICE OF MATERIAL

The working properties and characteristics of a material suitable for manufacturing any product are a very important part of material selection when designing products. Use should be made of data sheets and tables to ensure that the most suitable material is selected and that other constraints such as cost and manufacturing are considered.

The child's swing, which is shown on page 29 of the student book, uses steel tube for the main force bearing members of the frame. The frame must withstand both bending and torsional (twisting) forces. A table would have been used which lists the sections of steel available and how they compare when subjected to bending and torsional forces.

Examination question

Q1 *Explain **two** reasons why a large round section tube was selected to make the children's swing frame.*

4 marks

Acceptable answer

This type of material is the most **torsionally stiff** and will **stand up to the twisting forces** exerted upon it by the swinging motion of the child on the swing. It is also very **resistant to bending** and will be able to **withstand the flexing** resulting from the weight of children sitting on the swing.

COMBINING MATERIALS TO IMPROVE PROPERTIES

TOPICS

You need to understand:

☐ what an alloy is and why it is made

☐ how laminated materials are used to improve properties

☐ what composites are and how they are used.

KEY POINTS

WHAT IS AN ALLOY?

An alloy is made by combining two or more metallic elements together. Brass, high speed steel and solder are examples of alloys. The new material will have improved properties such as increased hardness, greater toughness or better resistance to corrosion.

LAMINATED MATERIALS

Laminating is a process that can be applied to:

• woods   • metals   • plastics.

A laminate is a single piece or sheet of material. When several pieces are stuck or bonded together they are said to have been laminated.

COMPOSITE MATERIALS

A composite material is a material made from one or more substances.

Composite materials are:

• MDF   • GRP   • carbon fibre.

Composite materials often have enhanced properties such as:

• improved tensile strength   • improved toughness
• good resistance to corrosion   • good strength to weight ratio.

BRASS

• An alloy of copper and zinc
• Has good corrosion resistance
• Easily cast and turned on a lathe

HIGH SPEED STEEL

• An alloy of medium carbon steel with tungsten, chromium and vanadium
• Very hard and can only be ground
• Good resistance to heat
• Ideal for use as cutting tools, milling cutters and drills

SOLDER

- An alloy of lead and tin
- Has a very low melting point
- Used in the construction of circuit boards

LAMINATING

- Allows mechanical properties such as strength to be increased
- Allows curved shapes such as chair legs and backs to be made by bonding thin sheets together around a former
- Laminating brass and invar forms a bi-metallic strip, used in kettles and heating control mechanisms such as switches
- Laminating plastic sheets creates hard wearing chemical resistant surfaces
- Laminating glass strand matting and epoxy resins allows curved shapes to be formed with great mechanical strength

The process of laminating involves building up thin layers around a former to produce the desired shape or curve. This process is a deforming process. Thin veneers, or skin ply, are cut to the required shape making sure that the grain is following in the same direction, following the curve.

- Thin layers are glued together with PVA or cascamite
- The layers are trapped between a jig or a former
- The pressure is maintained until the adhesive sets
- For larger items a vacuum bag can be used

Examination questions

 *Give **two** different examples of a composite material.*

2 marks

Acceptable answer

GRP (glass reinforced plastic) and carbon fibre

 *Brass is an alloy of copper and zinc. Describe **two** properties of brass.*

2 marks

Acceptable answer

Brass has very **good resistance to corrosion** and it also has **good fusability** that makes it **very good for casting**.

FINISHING PROCESSES

You need to know:

☐ about the need for finishing processes

☐ the principles behind surface preparation

☐ about the range of finishing processes.

KEY POINTS

THE NEED FOR FINISHING PROCESSES

A wide range of finishing techniques and processes is available for woods and metals. Plastics generally require less finishing due to the nature of the material and the manufacturing processes involved.

Finishing and surface treatments are usually carried out for one or both of the following reasons:

- Aesthetics – to enhance the appearance of the material.
- Functional – to protect the material and to stop it from deteriorating and to prolong its useful life.

When choosing a finish it is essential to consider:

- which material is best suited to the application
- where it is going to be used
- when to apply the finish
- maintenance of the finish
- surface preparation.

SURFACE PREPARATION

Surface preparation is vital. Poor preparation will result in a poor finish and one which will not last for long.

A range of surface finishes is available for woods and materials, as shown below.

RANGE OF PROCESSES

Woods	Metals
Polishes:	Painting:
Wax	Enamels
French polish	Hammerite
Staining	Plastic dip coating
Varnish	Etching
Paint:	Plating
Oil-based	
Polyurethane	
Spray	
Preservatives	

POLISHES

The two most common forms of polish are wax polish and French polish. Both types of polish bring out the grain of timber.

Wax polish

Wax oil produces a dull gloss shine. It is made from bee's wax dissolved in turpentine to form a paste. It is applied to timber using a cloth. With the addition of a silicon wax or carnauba wax, the durability of the wood is greatly increased.

French polish

French polish could also be used in any of the situations above. It does, however, produce a much higher glossed surface and you are also able to change the colour slightly.

STAINING

Staining or colouring is used to heighten the natural grain of timber. It is very much a decorative finish and allows for an even application of colour.

VARNISH

Synthetic resins (plastic varnishes) produce a much harder, tougher surface. They are heatproof and waterproof and quite good at standing up to tough knocks. They are best applied in thin coats with a brush or spray. In between each layer, the previous one should be gently rubbed down with wire wool. Varnish should always be applied in the direction of the grain, in light, even strokes.

PAINT

Paint can be applied to both woods and metals. It is used to provide a decorative colouring and protective layer whether used indoors or outside.

PLASTIC DIP COATING

Dip coating is a process that is suitable for most metals. It is used for coating metal products such as hanging baskets, brackets, kitchen drainers and tool handles. The metal must first be thoroughly cleaned and de-greased before being heated in an oven to 180°C. It must be soaked at this temperature before being plunged quickly into a bath of fluidised powder. It should be left there for a few seconds while the powder sticks to the hot surface to form a thin coating. The object should then be returned to the oven, allowing the plastic coat to fuse and leave a smooth glossy finish.

PRESERVATIVES

Garden sheds, fence panels and commercially produced furniture are all treated with wood preservatives, such as creosote – a tar/oil-based product – which soaks deep into the surface where it forms a barrier against damp and the entry of water.

ETCHING

Etching is a finishing process that allows patterns and designs to be made on the surface of metal and glass.

PLATING

Plating is a finishing technique that is often used to give metals like brass and copper a coating of a more decorative durable material such as silver or chromium.

SELF-FINISHING

Plastics undergo very little surface finishing because they already tend to be resistant to corrosion and general surface deterioration. The finish achieved on products such as washing-up bowls, lemonade bottles and plastic drainpipes are all due to the manufacturing processes involved. The high quality of finish is mainly due to the very high quality of the mould. Texture can be added to the mould, and will appear on the final product such as the top of a fizzy drinks bottle. Colour and tone are easily changed with the addition of chemicals and dyes into the plastic material.

A number of manufacturing processes result in products requiring little or no finishing, other than perhaps removing any flashing or sprue pins.

These processes are:
- injection moulding
- die casting
- extrusion
- blow moulding.

SURFACE PREPARATION FOR METALS

- All surface oxides should be removed with emery cloth or wet and dry paper.
- They should then be de-greased with methylated or white spirit.

SURFACE PREPARATION FOR WOOD

- A plane should be used to produce a clean, smooth surface.
- Minor blemishes should be removed with glass paper.
- Always work in the direction of the grain.

Examination question

 Explain **one** reason why it is important to thoroughly prepare the surface of a metal component before spray painting.

2 marks

Acceptable answer

If the material is not prepared thoroughly, over a period of time the paint on the surface will be affected by the impurities underneath it. This may be in the form of surface oxides and **rusting which will eventually break through** and **damage the painted surface**.

You need to:

☐ be aware of the need for accurate and careful marking out

☐ understand how basic marking out tools are used.

KEY POINTS

MARKING OUT

Careful and accurate marking out is essential in the realization of a quality product or component. Thought must be given initially to the datum edges from which all the measurements must be made.

BASIC MARKING OUT TOOLS

Four basic measuring tools are used in the school workshop:
- steel rule
- steel tape
- micrometer
- vernier callipers.

Various squares are used to mark out right angles and 45 degrees:
- try square – used mainly on wood but can be used on plastics
- engineer's square – for use on metal but can be used on plastics
- mitre square – used for marking out 45-degree angles.

Dividers are used to mark or scribe a circle or arc on metal or plastic. In order to stop the point from skidding over the surface, a small indentation is made with a dot punch. A centre punch is used where a hole is to be drilled. This mark provides a starting point for the drill and stops it skidding over the surface.

The basic types of gauges are:
- marking gauge
- mortise gauge.

Both gauges are used for marking out on timber. When using gauges it is important that they are held firm against the edge of the timber.

MARKING GUAGE

A marking gauge is used for marking lines parallel to an edge which runs along the grain.

MORTISE GUAGE

A mortise gauge is used, as its name suggests, for marking out mortise and tenon joints. It consists of two pins which will mark two parallel lines. It is used in the same way as the marking gauge.

Examination question

 Explain the differences between a dot punch and a centre punch.

2 marks

Acceptable answer

A centre punch should be used when you want to use a drill. The mark area provides a good start for the drill and it **stops the drill from slipping and skidding over the surface**. A dot punch should be used when you are about to use dividers to mark out an arc. **The indentation made by the dot punch is smaller and less likely to be noticed.**

WASTING PROCESSES

TOPICS

You need to know:

☐ the term wasting and wasting processes

☐ about machine wasting.

KEY POINTS

The term wasting refers to a process that produces waste or unused material by either cutting bits out or cutting bits away.

Wasting processes include:

- sawing
- planing
- filing
- chiselling
- using abrasive papers
- turning wood and metal on a lathe
- drilling
- polishing
- milling.

Wasting may be carried out using hand tools – saws, planes, files, chisels, abrasive papers. Machine wasting includes wood and metal turning on a lathe, drilling, polishing and milling.

Sawing

Four basic saws are used in the school workshop:

- Tenon saw – the most common type used for cutting wood and all general joints but specifically for cutting the shoulders on mortise and tenon joints.
- Dovetail saw – smaller and finer teeth than the tenon saw making it ideal for finer work but essentially designed for cutting dovetail joints.
- Coping saw – used for cutting curves in wood and plastics. It has a thin replaceable blade which can be rotated in a frame.
- Adjustable hacksaw – also has a replaceable blade but is essentially used for cutting metal. Different blades are available with fine and coarse teeth. It is important when cutting that as many teeth are in contact with the work as possible.

Cutting tools – planing

Planes are used for planing wood flat and to size. Two basic planes are used in the school workshop: smoothing and jack planes.

When planing it is essential that:

- the plane is set correctly
- you plane in the direction of the grain
- when planing across the end grain, a piece of scrap wood is used to stop the side from splitting out, or you plane from both edges into the middle.

Filing

Files are used for removing small amounts of unwanted material. A flat file is for general purpose use. More specialist file types are available such as round, square and half round.

Two basic filing techniques are used:

- Cross filing is used for the rapid removal of waste.
- Draw filing is used to reduce the marks left as a result of cross filing. This method leaves a better, smoother finish. An even finer finish can be achieved by wrapping a piece of emery cloth or wet and dry paper around the file and repeating the action.

Wasting processes

41

Chiselling wood

Four basic chisels are used:

- Firmer chisel – general purpose with a square shoulder.
- Bevel edge chisel – bevelled edges allow access into corners and is especially useful for cutting dovetails.
- Mortise chisel – used for cutting mortises, it has a thicker blade section allowing it to take blows from a mallet.
- Gouges – curved blades used for carving.

Abrasives

Abrasive papers can be used on woods, metals and plastics:

- Glass paper is used on woods.
- Emery cloth can be used on metals and plastics.
- Wet and dry paper can be used on metals and plastics but it should always be used wet.

Any abrasive paper should be used around a cork block to ensure an even pressure is applied.

MACHINE WASTING

Wood and metal turning

Wood turning can be carried out:

- on a faceplate, or
- between centres.

Faceplate turning is carried out on an 'outside' spindle and items such as fruit bowls and circular vacuum forming moulds are made in this way.

Between centres allows for long pieces of wood to be supported and turned. Stair spindles and lamp centres are made in this way.

In metal turning, a centre lathe operates in much the same way as a wood lathe. The faceplate is essentially replaced by a chuck where the work is held. It is also possible to turn between centres.

The main turning operations on a centre lathe are:

- facing where the tool is moved at right angles to the work, facing the end
- parallel turning where the tool is moved parallel to the work piece
- taper turning where the tool is moved at an angle to produce a taper
- parting where a narrow tool is fed into the work piece to trim or cut the work piece from the stock bar
- drilling where the tailstock is used to hold the drill bit stationary and is wound into the rotating work piece
- knurling where patterned hardened steel wheels are pressed into the rotating work piece.

Drilling

Twist drills are the most commonly found bits in school workshops. They are used for producing holes in woods, metals and plastics. Larger holes can be created with hole saws.

Polishing

Polishing is often done on a machine where a compound-coated mop wheel rotates at high speed and the work is held firmly against the bottom half of the mop.

Milling

Milling can be carried out manually or by computer-controlled machinery. It can also be carried out vertically or horizontally but in both situations it is the work that is clamped to the bed and moved past the rotating cutter.

Examination questions

 Q1 Describe **two** ways of avoiding the end grain from splitting when planing across the grain.

2 marks

Acceptable answer

One way to avoid the grain splitting when planing across the end is to put a **piece of scrap wood against one edge** and hold it **tight in the vice up against the piece that is being planed**. A second way to stop the grain splitting is to **plane into the middle** from **each of the two outside edges**.

 Q2 State the name of the saw used to cut metal.

1 mark

Acceptable answer

Adjustable hacksaw

 Q3 Facing is a process that is carried out on a centre lathe. Describe the process of facing.

2 marks

Acceptable answer

Facing is the process whereby the tool is moved across the rotating work piece at right angles.

 Q4 State the **two** different turning operations that can be carried out on a wood turning lathe.

2 marks

Acceptable answer

1 Turning on a faceplate
2 Turning between centres.

DEFORMING PROCESSES

You need to know:

□ that there are three main deforming processes – laminating, bending and vacuum forming

□ how each process is carried out

□ why each process is suited to specific applications.

KEY POINTS

MAIN PROCESSES

A deforming process allows the material to change shape without a change in its physical state. There are three main deforming processes:

- laminating
- bending
- vacuum forming.

The three main material groups used in schools – wood, metal and plastics – can all be bent easily.

Wood can be bent or curved around a former by making a series of parallel saw cuts across the width of timber. This makes it easier to bend and create curved surfaces which can be fixed to a frame. This process is called kerfing.

Timber is bent to make chair backs and to improve the aesthetic appeal of products which can now have smoother, rounder curved surfaces.

Laminating
Laminating wood allows its mechanical properties such as its strength to be increased. Single wooden laminates are bonded together in a flat form to create plywood. Thin laminates can also be stuck together and trapped between a former to produce curved shapes such as chair backs or legs.

Bending
Sheet metal is easily bent using folding bars. The sheet metal is trapped between the folding bars and, in turn, is held in a bench vice. A rawhide mallet is used to fold and crease the material over.

Metal is bent to form boxes and trays whereas tubes are bent to make stronger structures such as table and chair frames.

Tubes are bent using a pipe bender and two part former:
- The appropriate sized former is set into the pipe vice.
- The tube is inserted.
- A former is placed over the top of the tube and tightened down.
- A large force is then exerted as the pipe is deformed around the former.

Bends in acrylic can be made using a strip heater or line bender. A current passing through the element or wire generates a localised heat which is sufficient to soften the acrylic. As it softens it can be bent into shape or held in a former until it cools.

Examination question

The diagram below shows an acrylic napkin holder.

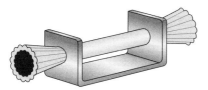

Describe how a former would be used to aid the batch production of 100 identical napkin holders.

4 marks

Acceptable answer

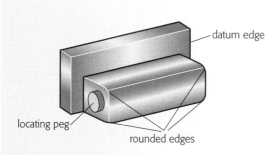

A former would be made which has **rounded corners** and a **locating peg** to make sure that the acrylic located in the correct space each time one was placed on it. The acrylic would be heated in an **oven until it was softened** and it would then be placed over the former and **held in place until it cooled**.

KEY POINTS

Vacuum forming

Vacuum forming is a process used to manufacture items such as Easter egg containers, chocolate box inners and shallow dishes and trays. Various materials can be vacuum formed, such as:

- acrylic
- ABS
- PVC
- Polythene.

The key issue with vacuum forming is the mould design and finish. Any imperfections on the surface will result in impressions on the surface of the final product.

Important features of the mould are:

- all vertical surfaces should be slightly tapered
- all sharp corners should be rounded off
- vent holes should be incorporated to avoid pockets of air becoming trapped.

The following statements refer to the stages of vacuum forming:

- The mould is placed on the bed and lowered
- The thermoplastic sheet is clamped around the edge with an air tight seal
- The thermoplastic sheet is heated up until it reaches a plasticized condition
- The bed is raised into the plasticized material and the air below is expelled
- Atmospheric pressure forces the plasticized sheet tightly over the surface of the mould
- Air is blown up into the formed sheet to help separate the mould from the formed sheet.

Examination question

The diagram below shows a simple desk tray made by vacuum forming.

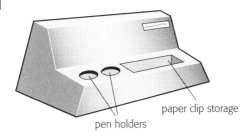

paper clip storage

pen holders

*Use notes and sketches to describe **two** features required in the design of a mould to produce the desk tray illustrated.*

4 marks

Acceptable answer

Two of the following:

1 tapered sides will allow the mould to be easily extracted
2 air holes to allow the trapped air to be expelled
3 rounded corners
4 filleted internal corners
5 a smooth finish is needed on the mould

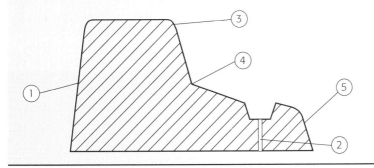

You need to know:

☐ that there are a number of fabricating processes

☐ that fabricating processes are temporary and/or permanent

☐ why each process is suited to specific applications

☐ about the use of jigs and templates.

KEY POINTS

Fabricating is the term used when different pieces or components are joined together to form a single product.

Tapping and threading provide a temporary fabricating process. They are used extensively in the joining of metals especially where bolts and machine screws are used.

Wood joints are permanent fabricating processes. It is essential to choose carefully the type of joint that is to be made. Since wood is a natural material, you must remember that it will continue to move. You should therefore try to make the joint as strong as possible and one way of achieving this is to make the gluing area as large as possible.

TAPPING

Tapping describes the process of cutting an internal screw thread. A tap is held in a tap wrench and it is turned clockwise to cut. Half a turn forward should be followed by a quarter turn backwards in order to break the swarf (waste metal).

THREADING

Threading is the cutting of an external screw thread and a die is held in a die stock and the cutting action is identical to tapping.

When threading, a chamfer should be filed on to the bar being threaded, but it is essential that the die is held square to the bar otherwise this will result in a drunken thread being cut.

TYPES OF WOOD JOINTS

- Butt joints – most basic form and the weakest since they only have a small gluing area

- Dowel joints – similar to butt joints but with a dowel used to reinforce it. The dowel adds extra strength as well as helping to increase the gluing area

- Halving joints – can be used on corners, to make tees or for cross halvings. Halving joints are made by cutting away half the thickness of the material on each piece

- Rebate joints – also known as a lap joint. One of the two pieces making the joint has a rebate cut into it which is normally half of its thickness

- Housing joints – can be cut in man-made boards as well as natural timbers and are most commonly used in the construction of cabinets for shelves or dividers. A stopped housing, as its name suggests, does not go right the way across the whole width of the board but stops just inside of the front edge
- Mitre joints – used on picture frames and skirting boards. The two pieces joining are cut at 45 degrees. Once glued they can be strengthened by the addition of pins
- Mortise and tenon joints – very strong and widely used in the construction of frames for furniture. The width of the tenon should be one-third of the width of the timber.

Examination questions

 A type of joint used in the construction of a chair is illustrated below.

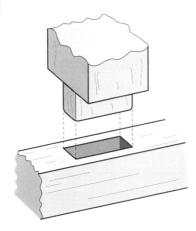

Name the joint illustrated above.

Acceptable answer

Mortise and tenon

 *Name **two** different tools which would be used to mark out the tenon part of a joint.*

2 marks

Acceptable answer

Mortise gauge and try square

KEY POINTS

Rivets

Rivets are permanent fabricating processes. They are extensively used with metal although they can be used to join acrylic and some woods to metal. Rivets are normally made from soft iron and come in a variety of head types and lengths.

Jigs and fixtures

Jigs and fixtures are one way of achieving a level of consistency in manufacturing. A jig is a work-holding device that is specifically made to hold a single component. The component would be held in an exact position but is free to be moved around.

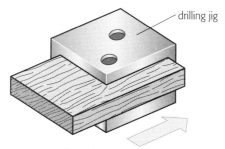

the timber is pushed into the drilling jig

Templates

Templates are used when a number of identical components have to be marked out. The template is often made from metal and it is used by placing it on the material to be marked out and either marking or drawing around its edges.

Templates are very useful when it comes to marking out complex and difficult shapes.

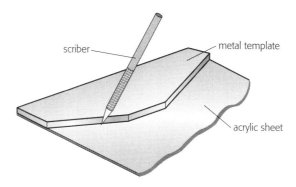

FABRICATING PROCESSES USING HEAT

All of the heat processes used for joining metal are permanent methods of fabrication.

Safety: any heat or welding equipment should always be used under supervision. Eye protection and protective equipment should be worn.

Whether brazing or soldering, a gas burning torch is used to provide the heat source and the severity of the flame is controlled by mixing gas and air together. A flux also has to be used with both joining methods. A flux serves two purposes:

- to prevent build up of surface oxides
- to aid the flow of solder or brazing spelter.

Thorough surface preparation is essential when brazing or soldering:

- The joint and surrounding area must be completely clean.
- A flux should be used.
- Start with a soft flame since a fierce flame may burn away the flux too quickly.
- The brazing spelter or solder should be melted on the hot metal, not in the flame.
- Once hot enough, time should be allowed for the brazing spelter or solder to flow.

Brazing as a process is only suited to joining mild steel whereas soldering can be used to make joints in brass, copper or tinplate. Tinning is a process where each separate piece being joined has a thin layer of solder applied to it. They are then brought into contact with each other and reheated or 'sweated' together. Whether brazing or soldering, sometimes separate components have to be held together in place with binding wire.

Welding is different to brazing or soldering in that the process involves melting and fusing together the pieces being joined rather than using a filler material.

Welding is a process that actually melts and fuses together the two pieces being joined, so that the joint is as strong as the original metal. Various methods exist but the most widely used methods in school are either electric arc or MIG welding.

Electric arc welding uses a large current to jump across a small gap. A current between 10 and 120 Amps is needed to generate the heat in order to melt the metal. A flux-coated filler rod acts as the current carrier and as it is burnt away during the welding process, the flux also burns away and protects the weld from oxidation.

MIG welding is similar to electric arc welding, but it benefits from a continuous feed of filler rod rather than having to replace it. An arc is struck between the work piece and the filler rod and an inert gas flows through the torch to prevent surface oxidation and slag from forming.

Examination questions

 *Describe **two** safety precautions which would be taken when carrying out any fabrication processes using heat.*

2 marks

Acceptable answer

Eye protection should always be worn especially when welding because of the **dangers caused by the intensity of the light**.

Tongs should always be used to remove work from the hearth or welding area because it **might still be hot**.

 *Give **two** reasons why a flux should be used when soldering.*

2 marks

Acceptable answer

Reason 1: To prevent the building up of surface oxides.

Reason 2: To aid the flow of solder around the joint.

You need to:

☐ understand the term reforming

☐ become familiar with reforming processes.

KEY POINTS

REFORMING

Reforming involves a material changing state from solid to a liquid or plasticised state and back again, during the manufacturing process.

Numerous reforming processes are used in the manufacturing industry, including:

- injection moulding
- casting
- die casting
- extrusion
- blow moulding.

PROCESSES

Injection moulding

The process of injection moulding is highly automated: that is, it involves little human intervention. As such, and because of the very high costs of producing the complicated moulds, the injection moulding process is only suitable for high-volume products such as washing-up bowls, buckets and many different household electrical goods cases. Injection moulding is best suited to thermoplastics although thermosetting plastics can be used.

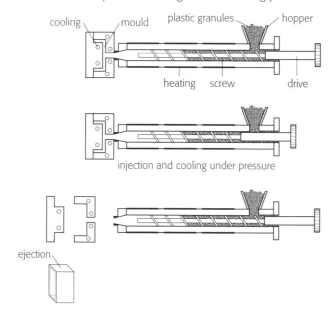

injection and cooling under pressure

The process of injection moulding can be broken down into the following stages:

1 The hopper is filled with granules.

2 The granules are heated by an element inside the machine.

3 A screw thread turns and pushes the softened material forward.

4 The plasticized material is then injected into the mould by a hydraulic ram.

5 Time is allowed for the material to cool and harden inside the mould.

6 The ram is withdrawn and the mould opens.

7 The moulded product is ejected from the mould by ejector pins.

8 The mould closes ready to make another product and the cycle continues.

Examination questions

 *Name **two** different reforming processes.*

2 marks

Acceptable answer
Injection moulding, casting, die casting, extrusion or blow moulding

xaminer's Tip

A question such as this has more than two correct answers. Any two correct reforming processes given will be marked as correct.

Q2 *Explain **one** reason why injection moulding is only suited to high-volume production.*

2 marks

Acceptable answer
Producing the moulds is very expensive and is therefore **not viable if only one product is required**. Thousands of individual components have to be made in order to recoup the cost of the mould.

Reforming processes

Casting

Casting is an ideal process for producing very complicated and detailed components from metal. Engine blocks and workshop bench vices are produced using this process.

The casting of aluminium in sand moulds is a relatively cheap and simple process which can be carried out easily in schools.

The process of casting can be broken down into five basic stages:

1 A pattern is made of the required piece.

2 The pattern is encased in sand in moulding boxes.

3 The moulding boxes are split and the pattern removed to leave a cavity.

4 Molten metal is poured into the cavity and left to solidify.

5 Once cooled, the work piece is removed and cleaned up.

Patterns can be either a single piece or a split pattern. All patterns should have a draft angle on all vertical surfaces, all external corners should be rounded off and all internal corners should be filleted.

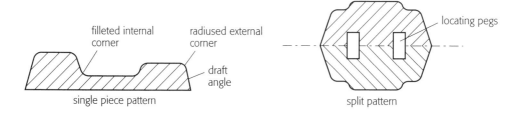

It is very important when casting that all risks are identified and assessed. Protective equipment should be worn and great care must be taken when pouring to avoid any spillages and splashes. Casting must always be carried out under the very strict guidance and supervision of a teacher.

Die casting

Unlike sand casting, die casting uses steel moulds or dies which are permanent. This means that the mould is made in many sections to allow the finished component to be removed.

Die casting uses lightweight aluminium and zinc alloys. As a result of the type of moulds used, die casting allows a high standard of detail to be achieved when moulding. The nature of the process also means that very little finishing is required except for removing any small amounts which have leaked out in between the die pieces. There are two types of die casting:

• gravity die casting

• pressure die casting.

The process of pressure die casting is similar to injection moulding in that the molten metal is injected under pressure by a hydraulic ram into a mould and left to cool before being removed from the mould.

Examination question

 Describe *two* differences between sand casting and pressure die casting.

Acceptable answer

Difference 1: Sand casting, as its name suggests, **uses sand to create the moulding** cavity whereas **die casting uses a permanent metal mould**.

Difference 2: **In pressure die casting the molten metal is injected into the mould under pressure** whereas in **sand casting, the molten metal is simply poured in under gravity**.

E xaminer's Tip

A full answer for 4 marks requires two separate differences to be identified and described.

Extrusion

All plastics undergo little secondary surface finishing because of the nature of the material and the manufacturing processes involved.

Extrusion is a process used to make uniform sections of materials such as drain pipes, hose pipes and guttering.

The plastic material is heated in the same way as injection moulding, but the screw thread rotates consistently pushing the plasticized material through a die. The shape of the die determines the shape of the extrusion profile. As a result of the smooth surface finish on the die, a high quality of finish is left on the surface of the extruded material.

Blow moulding

Blow moulding as a process is used to manufacture hollow products such as toy ducks, and containers for fabric conditioner and washing-up liquid.

A split mould is used which has a very high quality surface finish. This means that no other surface finishing is required other than printing or applying any labels. Texture can be moulded into products and this is done by machining the required texture on to the surface of the mould.

Fizzy drink bottles are made using a special process known as injection blow moulding.

Die casting, blow moulding, injection moulding and extrusion are only suited to high-volume production runs. They are all expensive processes to operate due to the initial costs of producing the moulds.

You need to know:

☐ what contributes to the quality of manufacture

☐ about the difference between quality control and quality assurance

☐ about the importance of tolerance.

KEY POINTS

QUALITY OF MANUFACTURE

The overall quality of manufacture is dependent upon a number of factors but it is recognized internationally by companies being awarded the International Standard of Quality ISO 9000.

QUALITY CONTROL AND QUALITY ASSURANCE

Quality of manufacture is monitored and maintained by quality control and quality assurance procedures.

Quality assurance is concerned with the overall process which includes the whole design process and regulating of suppliers to make sure they too conform to the ISO 9000 standard of quality.

Quality control is more concerned with the manufacturing aspects and the checking of actual products and individual components. Quality control is carried out by inspection and testing. Inspection looks at and examines various factors such as:

• dimensions   • appearance   • surface finish.

TOLERANCE

The tolerance of a component is the amount of imperfection that can be allowed on its dimensional accuracy. Some components within a product will have to be manufactured to a very high tolerance.

A shaft might have a diameter of 20 mm in diameter with a tolerance of $+$ or -0.05 mm. This shaft may have to fit into a bearing and so its dimensions are critical. With such a tolerance, the shaft can be bigger or smaller by no more than 0.05 mm. This means it could be 20.05 mm or 19.95 mm in diameter. If the shaft falls outside this tolerance, then the component would be scrapped. This aspect of checking components is part of quality control.

Another aspect related to quality control and the inspection of components is sampling. Once a batch of components has been completed, 50 for example, a quality control inspector will take a sample of shafts at random from the batch. The sample will be checked rigorously with accurate measuring equipment or with the use of gauges such as the YES/NO gauge. These measurements would be recorded on a chart and any which fall outside the upper or lower tolerance limit are rejected.

Sampling is undertaken:
• to check different batches of material
• to check different machine operators
• to check and guard against tool wear.

Examination questions

 Q1 *Describe how a tolerance gauge would be used to check the diameter of a circular component with a diameter of 10 mm and a tolerance of + or − 0.1 mm.*

Acceptable answer

A YES/NO gauge would be used. If the component **fitted inside the lower limit of the gauge or did not fit inside the upper limit**, then it would be **outside the tolerance range and it would be rejected**.

 Q2 *Explain the meaning of:*

a *quality assurance*

b *quality control.*

Acceptable answer

a Quality assurance is concerned with the International Standards that apply to the **whole process of design, suppliers and through to despatch and delivery**.

b Quality control is concerned **with the actual checking and testing of components while in the production and manufacturing stages**.

You need to know:

☐ about safe working practices

☐ how to recognize workshop hazards

☐ how to assess hazards and risks.

KEY POINTS

SAFE WORKING PRACTICES

When carrying out work in the school workshop, it is important to keep the working area clean, tidy and well organized. Always follow safe working procedures when using machinery or tools, such as wearing goggles, and make sure that you use the appropriate tools and machines.

Most accidents in the workshop result from carelessness. The best way to prevent them is to create and maintain a safe working environment. Make sure you know:

- what to wear
- how to behave
- how to work safely
- how to maintain your working environment
- what to do in the event of an accident.

Personal protective equipment (PPE) should be worn when provided and should always be worn when operating any machinery such as drills, lathes or sanding equipment. PPE includes gloves, breathing apparatus or masks, ear defenders and eye protection.

Always follow general machine precautions. If guards are fitted, such as those on drilling, milling machines and centre lathes, they should always be used. The area around the machine should be kept clear and only the person using the machine should operate the controls and the on/off buttons.

WORKSHOP HAZARDS

One way of preventing accidents is to know how to recognize hazards and to assess risk. A hazard is anything that might cause harm or damage. The actual possibility of a hazard causing harm or damage is known as the risk. A risk assessment is the study of the hazard and an assessment of how great the risk of that hazard is.

ASSESSING HAZARDS AND RISKS

To carry out a risk assessment, you need to look at the tools and processes involved and how likely they are to cause injury to the user or to others around them. For example, when using power extension leads, make sure that no one can trip or fall over them.

Risk assessments have to be carried out before any machine can be used. Sometimes your teacher will have done this and will then tell you about the potential hazards and the risk. Once a risk assessment has been carried out, it is sometimes necessary to put measures in place to control or reduce the risk. These measures and actions will lower the chances of any harm or damage occurring.

Examination questions

 Name **two** different pieces of personal protective equipment that should be used when sanding MDF on a centre lathe.

2 marks

Acceptable answer

Eye protection and breathing apparatus or a mask

 Explain what is meant by the term risk assessment.

2 marks

Acceptable answer

Risk assessment is the term associated with the **study of a hazard** and an **assessment of how great the risk of that hazard is**.

ICT AND ITS USE IN PRODUCT MANUFACTURE

You need to know:

☐ how ICT, including CAD, is used to generate, develop, model and communicate design proposals in single item production

☐ how ICT, including CAM, is used in single item production.

KEY POINTS

ICT and CAD/CAM can be used in many ways in the production of single items, and a variety of hardware is available in manufacturing.

CAD

CAD is used in the generation, development, modelling and communication of ideas. Hardware such as scanners and digital cameras enable the capture of images while clipart libraries, available on CD-ROMs and over the Internet, offer starting points in the development of graphical images.

A wide range of CAD software is available such as ProDeskTop, Techsoft, Corel and the Adobe suite. All of these can be used to create and modify design proposals. Printers and XY plotters can then be used to produce copies of designs.

CAM

With the development of more powerful computers and CNC machinery, CAM is used extensively for the production of single items and of products or components in high volume. Vinyl cutters can be used to cut graphics for products and milling machines and lathes are now controlled by bench-top computers. Such machinery is driven directly by the CAD software which was used to generate the designs. Simple or complicated 2D and 3D images modelled on screen can be output and produced in resistant materials using such machines.

Examination questions

 *Name **two** different pieces of CAD-based hardware.*

2 marks

Acceptable answer
Digital camera, scanner, XY plotter, printer

 *Give **two** advantages of using a CAD package for the generation and development of a design proposal.*

2 marks

Acceptable answer
Advantage 1: Changes, whether minor or significant, can be made quite easily and saved.

Advantage 2: Different features can be changed easily and viewed such as key dimensions, the colour or even surface texture.

ICT AND THE USE OF CAD/CAM IN BATCH AND VOLUME PRODUCTION

You need to be aware of:

☐ how CAD/CAM is used in batch and high-volume production

☐ how production lines and assembly lines are simulated

☐ how computer systems enable fast communication systems.

KEY POINTS

CAD/CAM IN PRODUCTION

The introduction and development of CAD/CAM has allowed manufacturing companies to develop highly automated and complex machinery. Once the machines have been set up and tooled, they can run non-stop and produce components in high volume. They can also be used to produce a batch of components or products before being reset and set up to run another programme.

Computer programs can be used to simulate assembly and production lines, allowing production engineers to assess how long a particular product or component will take to make. The programs also help engineers to work out the stages that manufacturing should take place in so as to make the best use of time, money and machinery. Simulation programs enable engineers to look at machining times when using CAM and also to look at the tool path and the clearance needed for the various machine tools involved, which allows them to work out where the material needs to be clamped.

COMMUNICATION SYSTEMS

Communication systems have advanced at a rapid rate in recent years and continue to improve. Computer networks now exist in almost every working environment, from major manufacturing companies to the smallest retail chain. By connecting computers to the Internet, using a modem, emails and faxes can be sent and received.

THE INTERNET

The World Wide Web (www) is the public face of the Internet. It is a huge collection of websites made up from individual web pages. The graphic images and text you see on a screen make up part of a web page.

Web pages are usually written in a language called HTML (hyper text mark-up language). This allows pages to be joined together to form a collection of pages to be joined together to form a website. One website can be linked to other sites around the world to form a global world wide web of connected sites.

The Internet is an almost unlimited resource bank with huge amounts of information and data accessible to all. It is a very useful tool to use when working on projects. It is also very useful for businesses to keep up to date on what their competitors are doing.

Most web sites can have e-mail links built into them so that you can contact the companies at the click of a button. This might allow you to request some information or a sales brochure.

E-MAIL

E-mails are sent at staggering speeds and at relatively low costs in comparison to faxes and the postal system. The only cost involved is the price of a short local telephone call. One of the major advantages of e-mail is its speed and response times. Another advantage is that documents, spreadsheets, drawings and CAM data can be sent as attachments to an e-mail so enabling information to be sent and received quickly to and from anywhere in the world. Remember, when e-mailing you should use the correct terminology and language and it should be composed in the same way as a letter. Be professional with its presentation and ensure your spellings are correct.

EPOS SYSTEMS

Electronic point of sale (EPOS) systems are used to gather and record information about products. Each product has its own unique bar code that is either stuck or printed on to the product.

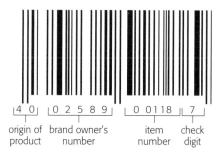

The code gives information about the country of origin, the manufacturer and the specific product code.

Companies use the information gathered by EPOS systems to:
- hold customers' and suppliers' details
- produce daily reports generated on sales or stock levels
- adjust and record stock levels
- order quickly and efficiently.

EPOS systems are also used within manufacturing companies to track and record components and products. They help with accountability and in the overall quality assurance and quality control procedures within the company.

Examination questions

 Q1   *Give **two** advantages to a company of having a website.*

2 marks

Acceptable answer

Advantage 1: A company can advertise their own products and services on the Internet.

Advantage 2: The company is also able to keep an eye on their competitors.

 Q2   *Give **two** advantages to the manufacturer of using an EPOS system.*

2 marks

Acceptable answer

Advantage 1: The manufacturer is able to access up-to-date information on stock levels.

Advantage 2: With up-to-date stock levels the manufacturer can adjust purchasing priorities in line with the latest sales information.

TOPICS

You need to know:

□ how CAD/CAM systems enable faster, more flexible manufacturing through:

   □ computer integrated manufacture (CIM)

   □ 2D modelling and creation of 3D 'virtual' products

   □ managing product design and design data

   □ production control via CNC equipment and automatic production.

KEY POINTS

CIM

Computer integrated manufacture (CIM) is used in the manufacturing industries for designing and making a variety of products.

CIM is a computer-driven control system which is used to integrate and link all aspects of CAD/CAM into the entire production process. The computers are linked into a network which controls the machinery and data relating to stock of completed products and of the raw materials and components.

The benefits of CIM:

- It is used to control highly accurate machinery carrying out repetitive processes.
- Results are consistent in quality.
- It can be used to produce high volumes of identical products or components quickly.

2D AND 3D MODELLING

CAD/CAM can be used to transform 2D images into 3D images on screen. This enables 'virtual' products to be created using powerful computer software and allows the product to be viewed from various angles. 2D design may well contribute to aspects of the packaging of products. 3D modelling saves time, and the software is capable of allowing us to see what the product looks like in various materials and in different colours.

CAM AND CNC

Computer-aided manufacture (CAM) is used to manufacture products and to monitor and control aspects of automatic production. Robotic materials handling devices and automatic guided vehicles (AGV) are examples of CNC equipment. They are used to 'pick and place' materials, move new material ready for machining or take away batches of completed work. Extensive use is made of feedback from electronic sensors within the machinery to ensure that quality is maintained such as:

- cutting speeds
- feed rates
- tool wear
- material handling components.

Use of CAD/CAM in manufacturing

Computer numerical control (CNC) means controlling the manufacturing and materials handling machinery by using numbers and codes generated by the computer's software. CAD and CAM software can be used to generate the machine codes and electronic data required to drive the CNC machinery such as lathes, milling machines and routers. This type of machinery is very expensive to purchase and set up but these machines allow for the fast, accurate and repeatable production of components and products in batches and in high volumes.

The advantages of CNC include:

- increased speed of production
- greater levels of accuracy
- increased flexibility from complex one-offs to batches and high-volume production
- the machines can operate continuously
- once set up and programmed, it is easy to operate.

Examination question

 *Explain **two** advantages of CNC equipment over manually operated machines.*   **4 marks**

Acceptable answer

Advantage 1: CNC machinery can be used to **increase the speed of production** because it **can operate continuously**.

Advantage 2: **Once it has been set up and programmed** CNC equipment can be used to produce products or components in **batches or in high volumes at great levels of accuracy**.

You need to know:

☐ that custom-made furniture made as a single item is known as a one-off

☐ that the target market group and the product specification will determine the level and scale of production

☐ that for larger quantities of products or components, batch or high-volume production will be used.

KEY POINTS

ONE-OFF PRODUCTION

The production of one-offs is often as a result of a customer's own design brief and specification. High levels of manufacturing skills and craftsmanship are used in the making of such products. Tools, machinery and equipment are general purpose and wide ranging. Products made as one-offs are often quite expensive in relation to similar products that have been either batch or volume produced. This is generally due to the amount of time taken to make the product and also reflects upon the skill level of the craftsperson.

Examples of one-off products include:
- specific aids for disabled people
- football stadiums
- bridges
- bespoke furniture for an office or home.

LEVEL AND SCALE OF PRODUCTION

The size of the target market and the scale of production will determine the type and range of manufacturing processes to be used in the product manufacture. However, large-scale machinery such as injection moulding machines and die casting machines are specially designed for specific tasks, even though different products can be made by changing the moulds.

Because this type of machinery is so specialized and can only perform a single function, its cost is high. This means that products to be made in high volumes or batches are ideally suited to this type of machinery. Products such as kettles, disposable pens and product casings are made in this way.

Two methods exist for larger quantity production: batch and high volume. The ultimate demand for the product will determine the level of production used.

BATCH PRODUCTION

Batch production is used when a fixed number of products is required at certain periods or periods of high demand. This type of processing requires the use of specialist machinery and the various components will be assembled on a production line. Once a batch has been completed, the moulds can be stored away and the machine prepared and set up ready to run another job.

Batch production is more economical than one-off production since greater amounts of materials are used which means a cheaper price can be obtained. Also, if moulds have been designed and made and large numbers are being produced, the cost of the mould and setting up of the machines can be recovered over a longer period so reducing the unit cost. Greater automation also means that fewer skilled workers are required.

Examples of batch-produced products include:

- vacuum formed Easter egg holders
- commemorative medals and coins
- a range of kitchen units for a new season.

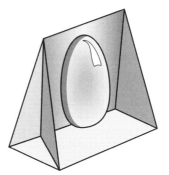

£5 coin for Golden Jubilee   Easter egg container

High-volume or continuous flow production uses highly efficient and automatic machinery. Identical products or components are produced continuously 24 hours a day, 7 days a week. This type of highly automated machinery is kept running and is only stopped when there is a problem such as a break-down or for servicing and repair.

High-volume production can be used in the production of:

- fizzy drinks bottles   • steel food cans   • CD cases.

Only a small workforce is needed, with one or two highly skilled machine setters and a few lesser skilled operatives, to maintain this type of production. The operators ensure the machines run smoothly and keep the machinery topped up with material such as the granules for injection moulding or extruding. To ensure safety and prevent accidents, the machines have guards.

Kettles are produced using injection moulding – a high-volume production process.

Examination question

 Q1 *Explain the difference between batch and high-volume production.*

4 marks

Acceptable answer

Batch production is used when a **fixed number of identical products** is required at **fixed times or at periods of high demand**. However, batch production can be carried out on machinery used for high-volume production. **High-volume production is continuous** and operates on **highly automated machinery**, 24 hours a day, 7 days a week.

xaminer's Tip

A full answer for 4 marks requires the differences to be identified and explained or justified.

Section 3
Assessment
objective 3

You need to be aware of:

☐ consumer issues such as the importance of product reliability and safety standards like:

- British Standards
- the BSI Kitemark
- the CE marking

☐ the development of modern and smart materials such as:

- carbon and Kevlar fibre
- piezo crystals
- metals which change length when subject to electric current – shape memory alloys.

KEY POINTS

CONSUMER ISSUES

Virtually every product has been designed and produced in response to a human need. Cars, televisions, mobile phones, furniture, kettles and CD players are all examples of product design. One kettle may be quite similar in function to another yet it might look quite different to another one which has been designed and made by another company. What is common to all kettles is a concern for the safety of the user and the reliability of the product.

Product safety and reliability are key issues for both the consumer and manufacturer alike. When we buy a new product, be it a car, television or stapler, we take its safety and reliability for granted because before a product gets to the retail stage, it will have been tested thoroughly for both safety and reliability. At times companies do get it wrong and products have to be recalled from the market place.

Any testing of products must be a fair test if comparisons are to be made with similar existing products. It is also important that testing is fair and consistent to ensure that similar products all conform to the same standards of both safety and reliability. For certain products, special pieces of testing equipment have to be designed and made.

Once a prototype has been designed and made, it will be tested by different people who might use it and in different environments and conditions. Independent safety inspectors will also carry out a series of tests on the product. Specific products and types of products have to conform to and pass very stringent British Standards (BS), for example:

- Medicine bottles
- Cycle helmets
- Children's toys
- Electrical products

In order to show consumers that products are safe to use and have passed the safety tests, special symbols are printed on the package or the product itself.

The BSI Kitemark shows that the product has been tested independently and that it conforms to or is above the standards expected by the British Standards Institution.

The CE (Certificate Europe) marking shows that the manufacturer has achieved the standards which were set down by the European Commission.

Examination question

 *Give **one** advantage for the consumer when buying a product which is displaying the BSI Kitemark symbol and **one** advantage for the manufacturer who can display this symbol on its products.*

2 marks

Acceptable answer

Advantage to the consumer: It will reassure the consumer that the product has been tested and is safe and reliable to use.

Advantage for the manufacturer: The indication that the product is safe is likely to increase its sales.

KEY POINTS

MODERN AND SMART MATERIALS

New materials are continually developing, such as carbon and Kevlar fibres. Carbon fibre and Kevlar are composite materials. This means that the fibrous material is held in a plastic thermosetting resin. Carbon fibres are used in much the same way as glass reinforced plastic (GRP). Carbon fibres exist in various forms such as:

- loosely woven fabrics
- filaments wound together in a string-like fashion
- matting consisting of short fibres
- loose short strands.

Carbon fibres and products made with carbon fibres are very strong and they have a high strength-to-weight ratio, that is, they are very strong in comparison to their weight. Carbon fibres are used for:

- golf club shafts
- tennis racket frames
- skis
- bike frames.

Kevlar is a composite material but it uses a special thermosetting polymer. It is used for some structural components in aircraft where it has led to the overall weight reduction of aircraft in recent years, especially in the military field.

Kevlar is also widely used in the production of protective clothing and body armour for the police and the armed forces. Kevlar is stronger and lighter than conventional carbon fibres but it is also more flexible. This has allowed body protection worn by the police to be much lighter and more comfortable, resulting in it being worn for longer periods.

Piezo electric crystals are used to make small electronic transducers. A transducer is a form of electronic output.

Piezo electric crystals can be used in two different ways. They can be used as either input or output transducers.

Input transducer	The piezo crystal will produce a voltage in response to a movement or a loud sound. In this mode, the transducer can be used in applications such as burglar alarms
Output transducer	In this mode, when a voltage is applied across it, the piezo crystal will produce a sound. It is used in musical greetings cards as the musical output transducer

polymer transducer   disc type   symbol for piezo-electric transducer

A metal whose length changes when an electric current is passed through it falls into a group of materials known as smart materials. The most common shape memory alloy is Nitinol, which is an alloy of nickel and titanium. This material has been heat treated to remember that at 70°C and above, it should be straight. If the wire is held tight, then when heated it will contract its length by 5 per cent.

Smart wires can be used to create mechanical movements in robotic applications. They can also be used as:

- greenhouse vents – to let hot air out
- bath mixer taps – to control valves on the hot and cold taps
- coffee makers – to open valves so that water at the right temperature drips on to the coffee.

TOPICS

You need to be aware of:

☐ moral issues such as changing fashions and planned product obsolescence

☐ environmental issues such as:

  – sustainable technology

  – forest management and pollution

  – dust and fume control

  – conservation of resources

  – waste management (reduce, reuse, recycle)

☐ influences of different cultures on design for manufacture.

KEY POINTS

MORAL ISSUES

Changing fashions, especially among young people, have a very important effect on the design, development and life cycle of products.

As one product becomes popular and fashionable, its sales increase until another product enters the market. At this point, its sales decrease and it becomes less popular.

With some products it is very easy to change the appeal quickly, reflecting new fashions and the faddish 'must haves'.

For example, a child's plastic lunch box is a product that can have its appeal changed very quickly to respond to changes in fashions and trends. The box itself does not change but the sticker is replaced to reflect the latest trend.

In today's constantly changing society, products can quickly become out of date or obsolete due to technological advances. On the other hand, some products are designed to be used just once or for a short period of time only, for example ballpoint pens, disposable razors and single-use cameras. When their useful life is over, or in most cases before, they are thrown away. This is called planned product obsolescence. The product will have a short life cycle.

The computer industry is another good example of where products are designed with a limited life or planned obsolescence. Advancing technology has meant that as soon as you buy a new computer, a newer, more powerful one is available almost immediately.

Examination question

 Many products are now designed with 'planned product obsolescence'.
*Give **one** advantage to the manufacturer of such products.*

2 marks

Acceptable answer

Such products result in greater turnover of products for the manufacturer
which means that its profits will be greater too.

KEY POINTS

ENVIRONMENTAL ISSUES

Environmental issues have gained much attention in today's technological society. As
manufacturing industries have increased output to meet consumer demand, an
ever-increasing demand has been placed on the world's natural resources. Designers,
manufacturers and consumers all have an important role to play in providing 'green' or
environmentally friendly solutions in order to sustain the world's natural resources.

Sustainable technology involves:

- the recovery of materials
- recycling materials
- reusing materials.

Forests need to be carefully managed and maintained to ensure that not too much woodland
is being felled or cut down. New trees also need to be planted in big enough quantities to
ensure that stock levels are maintained.

Infected and weak stock is also cut down and careful planting and felling ensure that each tree
has enough light and space to grow at maximum speed.

Wooden products which are made from timber from a managed forest now carry a stamp to
indicate this.

As manufacturing levels and energy demands have increased, so has the waste and pollution
generated. Fumes and gases ('acid rain' for example) have damaged the environment.

The European Commission and the UK government have introduced very tough controls, such
as the Control of Substances Hazardous to Health (COSHH) Regulations, to make factories
reduce their levels of emissions.

RECYCLING

Most materials can be recycled. This helps to save energy and to reduce pollution. It also means
that less new 'raw' material will have to be cut down or extracted from the earth and processed.

One of the disadvantages of recycling however is the scale of recovery. Without sufficient
quantities to recycle, the whole process becomes too expensive.

Recycling schemes are now commonly found in supermarket car parks. This allows for the
recycling of glass, paper, textiles and some metals.

Recycling is only viable if the recycled material can be integrated back into the manufacturing
chain and turned into products that consumers will buy in sufficient quantities.

COSHH REGULATIONS

The Control of Substances Hazardous to Health (COSHH) Regulations help to limit the amount of fumes and dust in the workshop. Where a risk has been identified, either to the workforce or the environment, careful measures and action have to be taken to reduce the risk. This can be in the form of dust and fume extraction systems.

Examination question

 *Explain **two** advantages of recycling to the environment.*

4 marks

Acceptable answer

Advantage 1: The more material which is recycled means that **less waste has to be dumped in landfill sites** or sent for incineration which results in less pollution.

Advantage 2: If materials are recycled and introduced back into the materials chain, **then less new 'virgin' material needs to be extracted and processed so saving both the natural resources and energy**.

KEY POINTS

One of the prime concerns of all designers should be to try to reduce and minimize the amount of materials used in their designs. The benefits of this are wide ranging and include:

- conservation of resources
- reduction in energy consumption
- less pollution
- reduction of waste for disposal and recycling.

One area where reductions can be made is in the packaging of products. Several layers and sometimes different materials are involved, all of which have to be disposed of.

In other instances, some supermarkets are operating refill schemes in an attempt to promote the reuse of plastic bottles and containers. Once the bottle is empty, it is taken back to the supermarket and refilled, therefore saving the plastic bottle. Paper and cardboard are recycled widely and the level of production has increased immensely in recent years. Toilet tissue, newsprint and corrugated board make extensive use of recycled paper fibres.

Examination question

 *Describe **one** advantage for the consumer in using the bottle refill system at supermarkets.*

2 marks

Acceptable answer

Since the customer is reusing the plastic bottle, they **will only be paying for the contents** and not the packaging, therefore they will be **saving money as well as reducing the demand for the outer packaging**.

Impact of values and issues on design and manufacture

INFLUENCES OF DIFFERENT CULTURES

There are many aspects that have to be considered when designing any product – for example, function is a key issue as is its aesthetic appeal.

If products are to be exported around the world, then careful consideration must be given to the cultural aspects of the product and the countries to which it is being exported. People of different cultures have different views and opinions on what is aesthetically pleasing and how products might function. Often these views are based on historical and religious images or works. It is, therefore, important for designers to be aware of both cultural and artistic influences on their work as well as the overall design for manufacture.

In recent years Japan has established itself as a technological superpower exporting goods all over the world. Electrical products manufacture has miniaturised, reflecting the simplicity, compactness and precision of the Japanese way of life and culture.

The major electrical companies such as Sony, JVC and Panasonic have created and developed a range of gadgets which have been designed and marketed as 'must haves'.

As design has developed, it has been influenced by many artistic and cultural trends. Many of these influences have been driven by the music industry and we have seen this reflected not only in the music itself but also in the clothing industries, such as punk, rap and the new romantics.

As designers create new products, they must consider the cultural, social, moral and environmental issues in relation to the products they are designing and where in the world they are going to be used.

Section 4
Advice on design and product analysis questions

This section contains advice on how to answer:

- design questions (not short course)
- product analysis questions.

KEY POINTS

- The design questions on the foundation tier and higher tier will be different.
- Full course paper: The product analysis question for the full course paper will be the same on both foundation and higher tiers. It will appear as question 4 at foundation and question 1 at the higher level.
- Short course paper: The product analysis question will be the same on both foundation and higher tiers. It will appear as question 3 at foundation and question 1 at the higher level.
- Both the design question and the product analysis question will be divided into smaller part questions which use the same key words as listed in Section 1. The type of answers required also follow the same pattern as the examples given in Section 1.
- The way in which these two questions differ from others on the paper is that each will focus completely on a single product, that is, all 22 marks.
- The products used for each question will be different and will be introduced at the beginning of the question.
- Both questions will test your ability to apply knowledge and understanding, of the Specification content, to the identified product.

DESIGN QUESTIONS (NOT SHORT COURSE)

The design question will test your ability to produce two different, relevant and viable initial designs from a given specification. You must apply your knowledge and understanding gained from studying the following topics of Design and Technology: Resistant Materials Technology to the production of your designs.

(a) Selection of materials and components:
- material form and intended manufacturing process
- functional properties of materials
- choice and fitness for purpose of materials and components.

(b) Processing and finishing materials:
- combination/processing of materials to create more useful properties
- functional properties of finishes – physical and visual.

(c) Manufacturing commercial products:
- manufacturing processes suited to the specified production volume.

(d) Design and market influence:
- environmental, moral and safety issues relating to material selection
- ease of manufacture of your design.

The following bullet points show the type of information given in each design question, supported by examples of wording. Each example is accompanied by brief explanations to help you identify the important things to consider and include in an answer. An example of a full design question with a model answer is included at the end of this section.

Each design question includes the following:
- A brief description of the background to the design situation. For example:
  'A furniture manufacturer requires a new design for a rack to hold compact discs (CDs) in their cases.'

- A list of specification points that your design ideas must satisfy. Each of these points will contain two linked elements, both of which must be satisfied in each of your designs to score full marks. An example of one specification point is:

  'Hold 10 single CD cases securely.'

- The two linked elements to be included in your design ideas are: 'Hold 10 single CD cases' and *'securely'*.

- The instructions and marks available for each part of the question. For example:

 *In the spaces below use notes and sketches to show **two** different designs of your product which meet the specification above.* **(2 × 8 marks)**

Key words

'Use notes and sketches': your answer to the design question should be sketched and, where necessary, supported with notes that give descriptions and clarify the sketches by providing additional important information that cannot easily be shown by sketching.

---

 xaminer's Tip

You must look at the functional requirements of each specification point and present different methods by which those requirements are met in each of your two separate design ideas.

---

 xaminer's Tip

Remember, there can be many answers that all appear to be different for this type of question. However, all successful answers must satisfy the common specification points given in the question.

---

xaminer's Tip

In part **(a)** of the question, you should produce two different ideas to access both sets of 8 marks. This means your ideas must be technically different, not cosmetically different – that is, a different technical method by which the set design task is satisfied rather than just changing the colour or the shape. For example, the stability required in the base for a standard lamp can be created in technically different ways, that is:
- from a solid piece of flat material (shape is irrelevant)
- from a sectional bar, tube, or rod material formed or fabricated to a flat shape.

 *Three of the specification points are given below. Use these headings to evaluate **one** of your design ideas against the initial specification.* **(6 marks)**

xaminer's Tip

Remember the key word 'evaluate'. This means that one or two sentences are required where the suitability or value of your idea is judged. It can include both positive and negative points, with each point being linked to a feature of your design and being supported with a valid justification or reasoning.

xaminer's Tip

The evaluation you carry out here should result in your giving the examiner new/additional information relating to how well your design is likely to succeed or why it might fail or need further development. This new information will be contained in these judgements and their justification or reasoning. It will probably be in the form of an *explanation*; simply repeating information previously *described* in part **(a)** of your answer will not score marks here.

xaminer's Tip

Remember to divide the time you spend on this question in proportion to the marks available for each part, that is:
(a) design idea 1 **(8 marks)** – approximately 8 minutes
(b) design idea 2 **(8 marks)** – approximately 8 minutes
(c) evaluation **(6 marks)** – approximately 6 minutes.

Example design question

A furniture manufacturer requires a new design for a rack to hold compact discs (CDs) in their cases.

The specification of the CD rack is that it must:
- *hold 10 single CD cases securely*
- *allow easy selection of the individual cases*
- *allow the labels to be read easily*
- *be suitable for production in batches of 100.*

*In the spaces below use notes and sketches to show **two** ideas for the design of the product which meets this specification.* **(2 × 8 marks)**

Model answer

DESIGN IDEA 1

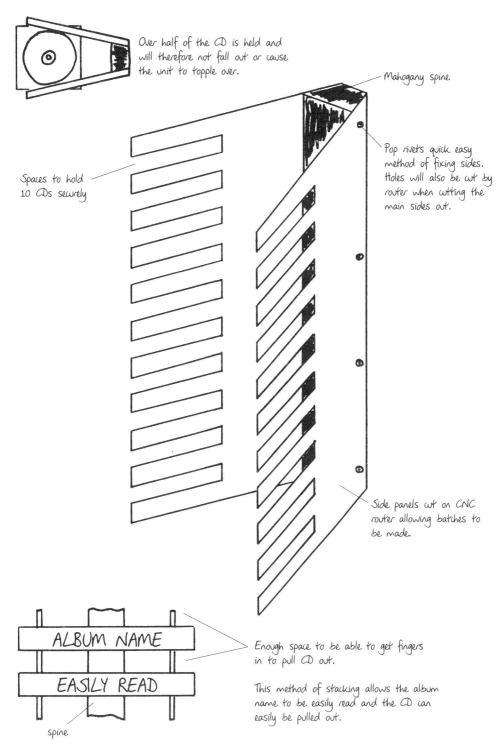

Over half of the CD is held and will therefore not fall out or cause the unit to topple over.

Mahogany spine

Pop rivets quick easy method of fixing sides. Holes will also be cut by router when cutting the main sides out.

Spaces to hold 10 CDs securely

Side panels cut on CNC router allowing batches to be made.

ALBUM NAME

EASILY READ

spine

Enough space to be able to get fingers in to pull CD out.

This method of stacking allows the album name to be easily read and the CD can easily be pulled out.

DESIGN IDEA 2

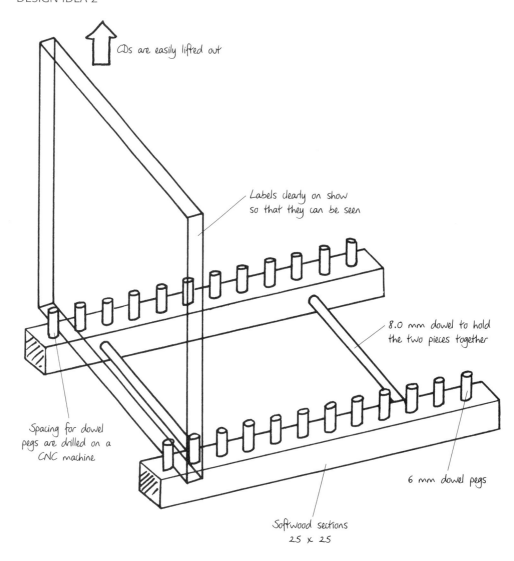

CDs are easily lifted out

Labels clearly on show
so that they can be seen

8.0 mm dowel to hold
the two pieces together

Spacing for dowel
pegs are drilled on a
CNC machine

6 mm dowel pegs

Softwood sections
25 x 25

PRODUCT ANALYSIS QUESTIONS

Each product analysis question will give information about a commercially produced product
in the form of:

- an illustration
- any additional data necessary for you to answer all part questions.

You will then be required to interpret this information and combine it with the knowledge and
experience gained from studying Design and Technology: Resistant Materials Technology to
answer the part questions set from any of the following topics:

(a) Selection of materials and components:
- the working characteristics of materials in relation to their function within the product
- the relationship of the material's final form in the product and the manufacturing process
- functional properties of materials in relation to their use in the product
- choice and fitness for purpose within the product of materials and components.

(b) Processing and finishing materials:
- combination or processing of materials to create more useful properties and how these have been used beneficially within the product
- functional properties of finishes – physical and visual – and why they are important to the product
- how the materials have been prepared for the manufacture of the product
- how and why pre-manufactured standard components have been used in the product
- where and/or why specified tolerances have been used in the manufacture of the product
- how and/or why ICT has been used in the design and/or manufacture of the product.

 (c) Manufacturing commercial products:
- an awareness of a manufacturing process suited to the specified production volume for the product and an understanding of why it is suitable
- an awareness of how ICT, including CAD/CAM, is used in batch or volume manufacture of the product.

(d) Design and market influence:
- evaluate the quality of design and quality of manufacture in terms of the product performance criteria related to the following – function, the needs and values of users, moral cultural and environmental considerations, the materials and processes used, safety and value for money
- consider the design features that make the product suitable for manufacture in the specified quantity
- planning of production for the product including production schedules, quality control and quality assurance.

(e) Give and justify points of specification for the given product.

xaminer's Tip

Remember, not all of these topics will be covered each year and just because a topic was covered in a previous year does not mean that it will not be included again.

Examiner's Tip

Key words

Remember, the type and complexity of answers required to any part question is shown by the use of the key words used in the question, that is, Give, State, Name, Describe, Explain, etc.

Example questions

The following are examples of part question types that may be included in product analysis questions. Each part question is linked to the product described in the introduction.

For this example, the question would start by showing an illustration of an unopened plastic mineral water bottle complete with its screw top.

Two points of specification for the bottle and its top are:
- *it must hold the drink hygienically*
- *it must be easy to hold for opening and pouring.*

   *Give **three** more points which must be included in the specification for the mineral water bottle and its top. For each point give a reason why it must be included.*

1 ....

Reason ....

2 ....

Reason ....

3 ....

Reason ....

(6 marks)

A full answer for 6 marks requires three valid points of specification for the product, each linked with a valid reason for its inclusion, for example:

1 It must be made from **non-toxic materials** because the **food product must not be contaminated**.

2 The top must have a **tamper evident function**, because the **consumer must know that the product has not been opened** before purchase.

3 The **top must reseal** because the food product **may not be consumed at a single opening** of the bottle/the **remaining food product must be stored hygienically** and to **preserve its quality** for as long as possible. (Note: this answer has three alternative reasons.)

Examiner's Tip

Note that each of the answers is given in two parts – the point of specification followed by the reason. The two parts are linked by the word 'because'.

Another key word may be used in this question – 'Complete'. For example:

 Q4 *The screw top of the mineral water bottle is made from thermoplastic. It is to be injection moulded in batches of 100,000.*

*Complete the block diagram below to show, in the correct sequence, **four** more main stages of the injection moulding process.*

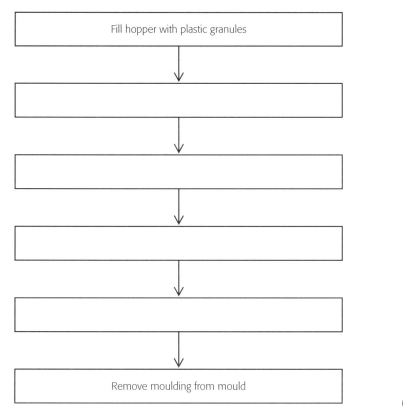

Fill hopper with plastic granules

Remove moulding from mould

(5 marks)

A full answer for 5 marks requires four main stages to be written in the spaces provided, and in the correct sequence, for example four from: clamp mould in machine; heat granules until soft; inject soft plastic into mould; allow soak time for moulded plastic to freeze (solidify); release mould from clamp. You would receive 4 marks for the main stages and 1 mark for the correct sequence.

xaminer's Tip

Note that the wording of each stage in the question is a brief phrase. This is a guide to show the detail required in the answers; each stage of the answer given above is a brief phrase – single-word answers will seldom give enough information to fully identify an individual stage and earn the mark.

Revise for Edexcel GCSE: Graphic Products

The best preparation for the exams

This new revision guide has been endorsed by Edexcel and is written to exactly match the specification by an experienced Edexcel examiner. It is designed to reinforce exactly what students need to know for the exam, and is suitable for both the long and short course.

Each guide contains:

- activities to make sense of what students have learned in class;

- tests and practice exam questions with answers for extra practice;

- key words and definitions to make sure students are fully aware of the technical vocabulary required;

- advice on answering different types of questions students may encounter in the exam

- tips and guidance on what examiners are looking for from the answers;

- summaries of key information to help identify the main points;

- a clear indication of what information is only tested in the short course, so students can focus on what is relevant;

ORDERING INFORMATION
Revise Edexcel Graphic Products
0 435 41721 5 • £5.99

SERIES EDITOR
Chris Weaving is the Chair of Examiners for Edexcel.

AUTHOR
John Halliwell teaches Graphic Products at Hirst High School, Northumberland and is a GCSE examiner for Edexcel.

S 302 ERB A

GCSE Graphic Products for Edexcel

Endorsed by Edexcel and matched to the specification

GCSE Graphic Products for Edexcel has been written to give students a solid understanding of Graphic Products at GCSE level and prepare them thoroughly for their coursework and examination.

This Student Book is suitable for the long and short course and includes:

- practice exam questions to familiarise students with the format of the exam;

- practical activities for students to practise what they have learned;

- advice and guidance from the examiners, so students know what is expected;

- clear indications of what material applies to the long course so students only need to cover what is relevant to them.

An accompanying Teacher's Resource Pack containing photocopiable materials and guidance on teaching the course is also available.

ORDERING INFORMATION
GCSE Graphic Products for Edexcel
0 435 41780 0 • £13.50

AUTHOR
Jon Attwood is a paper reviser for Graphic Products for Edexcel and was on the team that developed the current GCSE specification. He is ideally placed to ensure quality materials and thorough coverage of the specification.

Inspiring generations

S 302 ERG A2

GCSE Resistant Materials Technology for Edexcel

Endorsed by Edexcel and matched to the specification

These are the only resources available written specifically for the Edexcel GCSE in Resistant Materials. *GCSE Resistant Materials for Edexcel* gives students the best preparation for their coursework and exams and supports Foundation and Higher level students.

This Student Book is suitable for the long and short course and includes:

- practice exam questions to familiarise students with the format of the exam;

- Practical activities for students to practise what they have learned;

- Advice and guidance from the examiners, so students know what is expected;

- Clear indications of what material applies to the long course only, so students cover what is relevant to them.

An accompanying Teacher's Resource Pack containing photocopiable materials and guidance on teaching the course is also available.

ORDERING INFORMATION
GCSE Resistant Materials for Edexcel
0 435 41783 5 • £13.50

AUTHOR
Barry Lambert teaches Resistant Materials at Cheltenham College and is an experienced author and examiner for Edexcel. He is ideally placed to ensure high quality materials and thorough coverage of the specification.

Inspiring generations

S 302 ERG A1